NUMBELIEVABLE!

THE DRAMATIC STORIES BEHIND THE MOST MEMORABLE NUMBERS IN SPORTS HISTORY

SPECIAL COMMENTARY BY
DICK VITALE

MICHAEL X. FERRARO AND JOHN VENEZIANO

TRIUMPH
BOOKS

Library of Congress Cataloging-in-Publication Data

Ferraro, Michael, 1967–
  Numbelievable!: The dramatic stories behind the most memorable numbers in sports history / Michael Ferraro and John Veneziano.
     p. cm.
  ISBN-13: 978-1-57243-990-0
  ISBN-10: 1-57243-990-4
1. Sports-Miscellanea. I. Veneziano, John, 1964– II. Title.

  GV707.F47 2007
  796—dc22

                              2007009861

This book is available in quantity at special discounts for your group or organization. For further information, contact:

Triumph Books
542 South Dearborn Street
Suite 750
Chicago, Illinois 60605
(312) 939-3330
Fax (312) 663-3557

Printed in U.S.A.
ISBN: 978-1-57243-990-0
Design by Nick Panos
All photos courtesy of AP/Wide World Photos unless indicated otherwise.

This book is for everyone who has beaten the buzzer, strung up goose eggs, broken the tape, run it up, been knocked down for the count, given the impossible 110 percent, batted a thousand, broken par, run the table, taken one for the team, left too many ducks on the pond, hoisted a low-percentage shot, double-faulted, lit up the scoreboard like a pinball machine, fried the radar gun, been double-teamed, drained a three-pointer, hit for the cycle, kept both feet inbounds, played the full 60 minutes, took the extra base, notched a hat trick, made a twin killing, hit the daily double, shot their age, picked up the 7-10 split, scratched on the 8-ball, tossed a 1-2-3 inning, run the 2-minute drill, laid one in right between the numbers, stuck the bull's-eye, smoked a 1-iron, held serve, burned off a power play, and perhaps most importantly, moved the chains on 4th and 26.

To my dream team: MA, Maddie, and Ryan.

—JV

For all those who've dished out big assists along the way—especially Catherine, Jayne, and my sweet T.

—MXF

CONTENTS

ACKNOWLEDGMENTS

With grateful appreciation to all the mentors, editors, and publishers along the way who have strived to make us better at doing what we do—Lindon Hickerson, Jon Regardie, Sue Laris, Ed Carpenter, Bill Cleary, Jack Grinold, Adam Scharff, and Josh Zimman. And a big hullabaloo to our Badger-loving agent Ian Kleinert, and kudos to everyone at Triumph, especially Mitch Rogatz, Tom Bast, Amy Reagan, and Linc Wonham.

Thanks, too, for sport-loving friendship, insight, support, and suggestions from the bleacher creatures who have been part of our lives: Steve Strobel, Norm Strobel, Butch Vig, Beth Halper, Clay Buckley, Rob Hammersley, Dave Rygalski, Lonnie Burstein, Bill Morse, Tony Strickland, Doug Battista, Pila Boyd, Stick Bielefeld, Brad Kalas, Mark Sarian, Kevin McCormick, Kevin Healey, Peter Berman, Bil Dwyer, Gary Leonard, Steve Hirsen, Chris Nagi, Dean Ellis, Bob Rogers, Sean Murphy, Jay Barry, Drew Ohlmeyer, Marc Riva, David Smink, Mike Coyne, Chris Pizzello, Jeff Rosenthal, Ray Artis, Erik Christenson, Patrick Byrnes, Al Hans, John Manz, Pat Laverty, Bill Burke, Ed McGrath, Dan Furlong, Pat Falla, John Dulczewski, Tom Moore, Sandy Burgin, Mike Sottak, Frank Cicero, Fran Toland, Bob Malekoff, Paul McNeeley, Jamie Weir, Chuck Yrigoyen, Brett Hoover, George Sullivan, Bernie Corbett, Doug Brown, Jon Meterparel, Frank Sullivan, Harry Parker, Tim Murphy, Roger Crosley, Don Benson, Steve MacDonald, and more members of the Ferraro and Veneziano families than we're able to count (but especially our parents).

An extra special thanks to the students and faculty of Cathedral High School of Los Angeles, and a very talented young writer named Gabriel Montes.

In crunching the numbers and getting the stories, here are some resources we found particularly helpful: baseball-almanac.com, baseball-reference.com, www.cbc.ca (for all sports Canadian), dodgers.com, nba.com, nfl.com, espn.go.com, sportingnews.com, baseballhalloffame.org, the *New York Times* and *The Boston Globe* archives, and *The Baseball Encyclopedia* (1993, Macmillan Publishing Company).

And finally, infinite thanks to all the players who piled up the numbers in the first place.

INTRODUCTION

When we first told friends and fellow sports fans about *Numbelievable*, their eyes lit up and almost instantaneously a number flew out of their mouths. "You mean like...56?" "...61?" "...100?" Yeah, exactly.

That's because if you're a true sports fan, you know numbers. They ride shotgun with practically every great sports memory. And all of us have our favorites. For old-timers and purists, it's numbers like 714 (Babe Ruth) and 49-0 (Rocky Marciano) that spring to mind. Baby Boomers point to 17-0 (the '72 Dolphins). The *SportsCenter* generation raves 7 (Lance Armstrong's Tour de France wins). When the premise of important sports numbers was mentioned to a class full of boys at Los Angeles's Cathedral High School, the response was a nearly pitch-perfect chorus of "81!" (Sorry, Kobe, but we'll find a way to get you into our second edition.)

For us—a pair of "Philly" guys who took to sports like salt to a soft pretzel—this has always been the case. When our paths first crossed in the 1980s while attending Boston University, we experienced an instant sports connection as we followed the athletic exploits of the Terriers and lamented the slow decline of our beloved 76ers.

Several years later, the idea for this book was born and number-crunching became our quest. This by no means stands as a comprehensive collection of all the magical and memorable numbers in sports. We humbly leave that task to the Great Scorekeeper in the skybox. Instead, we created specific categories and painstakingly whittled potential entries down to only those that linger, those that astound, those that carry that certain *je ne say hey*. To see what we mean, thumb through the chapters, simply reading aloud the numbers to a fellow sports fan. See how many they can "get" without any further clue.

Lots, we bet.

At the same time, there are probably dozens of digits that you simply cannot fathom did not make these pages. We feel your pain. So with condolences to -48, 1.12, 22, $252 million,* and countless others that didn't quite make the cut, we proudly present *Numbelievable*.

—*Michael X. Ferraro & John Veneziano*

**(Wind chill at the Ice Bowl, Bob Gibson's 1968 ERA, Bob Lanier's shoe size, and Alex Rodriguez's record-breaking contract.)*

I am thrilled to be involved with this book. It is really fascinating to take a look at numbers and the way they are used in sports.

When an athlete is "in the zone"—totally focused, mentally and physically prepared—he or she can put up special performances. Over the years, many athletes have recorded extraordinary efforts. What makes these performances special? There is the ability to rise to the occasion in a special situation. Oftentimes these memorable performances come on the big stage—at a major event, in a playoff, or for a championship.

Think about it. The crème de la crème can step it up and post incredible statistics in the pursuit of winning. They find a way to get to the winner's circle, to give that extra little push to do the extraordinary. These individuals have different levels of expectation, and then they live up to that billing.

Many of these were record-breaking performances. Some of them shattered marks that existed for years and years, and a few of them topped numbers that were considered unreachable until special athletes had other thoughts.

Thinking about some of them now, I don't believe that anyone is going to match Wilt Chamberlain's 100-point game in Hershey, Pennsylvania, in 1962, and I know his mark of 50.2 ppg in 1961-62 is out of this world. Then you see Kobe Bryant score 81 points against Toronto and you wonder if that magical century mark is attainable. All of a sudden the impossible seems reachable.

Being in the zone leads to greatness... truly remarkable stuff that you never expected to see. Greatness is the only word to use for Secretariat at the Kentucky Derby and later in the Belmont Stakes in 1973. The same can be said for a young Tiger Woods blowing away the field at the 1997 Masters. Mark Spitz was in the zone for his brilliant Olympic performance, an unmatched seven gold medals.

This chapter is about athletes that are awesome, baby, with a capital A!

Dick Vitale

LIGHTING IT UP

Numbers Straight Out of the Zone

WHEN YOU **TURN 21,** **-18**
YOU OFFICIALLY BECOME AN ADULT. AND
FOR **ONE IN SIX BILLION**, YOU
BECOME A **LEGEND**.

Tiger Woods

It was April 1997 and anyone who knew golf already knew the name Eldrick "Tiger" Woods. At age three, he appeared on *The Mike Douglas Show* smacking golf balls straight and long. He was just eight when he won his first tournament. At 15 he became the youngest player to capture the USGA Junior National Championship, then proceeded to win the event three straight times. From 1994 to 1996, while attending Stanford University, he claimed three consecutive U.S. Amateur titles. After the third win, Woods pined for new challenges and turned pro. He won twice on the PGA Tour before the season was done.

Impressive, yes. But the Masters was different. This is the place that invited—and then humbled—the world's best golfers. How would this youngster, who had played Augusta just twice previously and whose professional career had spanned all of eight months, withstand the rigors of the course or the weight of the moment? Come back in five years, whippersnapper.

Instead, over a four-day span, the 21-year-old Woods put on a show for all ages. He became the tournament's youngest champion—and its first African American (and Asian American) winner—by dominating the course and the competition in such overwhelming fashion that some suddenly concluded the 6,925-yard track was obsolete.

Of course, if Woods had come on the scene three decades earlier, he might have never had the chance to show his stuff at the Masters. Blacks were excluded from the field until 1972, when the PGA implemented a rule stating any golfer who won a PGA Tour event had to receive a Masters invitation. Lee Elder became the first black to compete at Augusta in 1975.

"I wasn't the pioneer," cautioned Woods after his victory. "Charlie Sifford, Lee Elder, and Ted Rhodes played that role. I said a little prayer and said thanks to those guys. Those are the ones who did it for me."

After closing out the tournament with a

14-foot birdie putt on Augusta's "Holly" hole, Tiger pumped his fist in triumph, fully aware of the history he had made. Both his score of minus-18 and his staggering 12-shot margin of victory over runner-up Tom Kite (are you still a runner-up if you've been lapped?) were Masters records.

Author John Feinstein compared the unprecedented accomplishment to "a rookie in baseball hitting .600."

Even the youngster's opening round at Augusta gave little indication of what was in store. Woods went out in a jittery 40 on the front nine before zoning in with four birdies to close his day at a 2-under-par 70, a figure that had him lurking in fourth place.

On Friday he made his move, shooting 66 and easing into first place. Saturday was showtime. On a day when the average score was a lackluster 72.2, Woods's 65 outclassed the field, putting nine strokes between himself and the nearest challenger, Constantino Rocca. Still, those cynics who dreamed of drama wondered aloud if Sunday would resemble the Masters of a year earlier, when Greg Norman squandered a 6-shot lead over Nick Faldo. Instead, Day Four was nothing less than a coronation—the awestruck crowds roared at the spectacle as young Woods coolly carded a 69.

Elder, incidentally, arrived in time to see Woods's triumph, making the 500-mile drive from Pompano Beach, Florida, on Sunday morning. "I would compare this to Jackie [Robinson]," said Elder after seeing Woods fitted with his 42-long green jacket. "To me, a black winning a major golf championship is just as high as that."

And, conversely, just as low as Woods's jaw-dropping score of -18. Tiger may have been green, but now he had the blazer to match.

THE YOUNGEST MASTER When 21-year-old Tiger Woods tamed Augusta in 1997, he became the youngest player to win the Masters.

1:59.4

A HORSE SETS A NEW STANDARD FOR A PRESTIGIOUS OLD RACE

Secretariat

Horses aren't machines. Not even thorough-breds, those beautifully designed, thou-sand-pound animals that race for the Triple Crown every year.

But Secretariat came close. Affectionately known as the Big Red Horse, the dominating winner of the 1973 Triple Crown kicked off the prestigious cycle of stakes racing that year with a magnificent performance, posting the first sub-2:00 clocking in the 99th running of the Kentucky Derby.

Ridden by jockey Ron Turcotte, who just the year prior had guided Riva's Ridge to victory in the Derby and the Belmont Stakes, Secretariat entered the race as the 3-2 favorite, but with serious questions about his ability to handle the distance of 1¼ miles. His sire, Bold Ruler, had produced winners, but only of one-mile-and-below races, and the Big Red Horse had faded in his warm-up race for the Derby, finishing third at the Wood Memorial behind stablemate Angle Light and the place horse, a new con-tender named Sham.

(Of course, race historians now know that Secretariat had a huge abscess inside his mouth, which caused him to not accept the bit and almost certainly accounted for a sub-par performance.)

In the Derby, Secretariat didn't lead wire to wire. In fact, he started out near the back of the pack, and Turcotte was content to let him find his groove. Smart move by the Hall of Fame jockey.

"He was really a push-button horse," said an admiring Turcotte. "Just like a car."

Responsive and ready, Secretariat kept up-shifting right on time for his rider, clipping off horses from the field of 13 one by one as the race wore on. His first quarter-mile time was an unre-markable 25⅕ seconds, but the next was a brisk :24, and the third was stronger still, at :23⅕.

Racing up on the outside and gobbling up real estate on the leaders, Secretariat's willful stride started to send a surge of electricity through the overflow crowd of 134,476. His fourth quarter was clocked at :23⅖. Sham, one of the horses that had bested Secretariat at the Wood Memorial, was proving that his name was a misnomer, holding onto the lead and tiring ever so slightly.

But tiring is a fatal mistake when you're up against a horse with an oversized heart.

According to the report from *The Daily Racing Form*, "Turcotte roused [Secretariat] smartly with the whip in his right hand, leaving the far turn, and Secretariat strongly raced to the leaders, lost a little momentum racing wide into the stretch where Turcotte used the whip again, but then switched it to his left hand and merely flashed it as the winner drew away in record-breaking time."

Thundering down the final quarter mile in 23 seconds flat, Secretariat flew past Sham, right into the winner's circle, into the record books, and into the hearts of the American people. Not only did the Big Red Horse clock the first-ever sub-2:00 Derby, but he also had pulled off the near-miraculous feat of reducing his time in each successive quarter mile. The clock had been rocked, and the stage was set for the rest of Secretariat's Triple Crown triumphs.

BIG RED WON
Secretariat, with jockey Ron Turcotte aboard, takes the 1973 Kentucky Derby by thundering home in a record-setting 1:59.4.

3:59.4

BY LESS THAN A SECOND, ROGER BANNISTER SET A RUNNING FIRST.

Roger Bannister

Exactly what was Roger Bannister chasing on the blustery afternoon of May 6, 1954?

History.

The 25-year-old Brit smashed one of sport's most daunting psychological and physical barriers that day on the Iffley Road track in Oxford, becoming the first man to run a sub-four-minute mile. A curious crowd of 3,000—most of them Oxford undergraduates—watched in awe as Bannister, competing for the Amateur Athletic Association in a meet against his alma mater, broke the tape in 3:59.4.

For eight years, Sweden's Gunder Hägg had owned the record in the mile with a time of 4:01.3, and some track cognoscenti began questioning whether the four-minute mark would remain as elusive as the Loch Ness Monster.

Oh, Nellie, it wouldn't, and that's because Bannister, born on March 23, 1929, in the London suburb of Harrow, solved the mystery. He had become an inspired and accomplished mid-distance runner after watching countryman Sydney Wooderson (a one-time world-record holder in the mile), and he competed for Great Britain in the 1952 Helsinki Olympics. Undaunted by a disappointing fourth-place finish in the 1500 meters at Helsinki, Bannister refocused his efforts on rewriting the record book. With that, the race was literally on between Bannister and his chief rivals of the day—American Wes Santee and Australian John Landy—to become the first to attain track's Holy Grail.

Aiding Bannister at Oxford were two pacesetters—friends Chris Brasher and Chris Chataway—but he still contemplated calling off the bid because of crosswinds that shot 25 mph gusts across the cylinder track. After much deliberation, he elected to make a run at it.

At the opening gun, Brasher shot to the front with Bannister following in his shadow. As they crossed the half-mile mark—with a 1:58 split and the record now a real possibility—Brasher faded and Chataway took the lead. Just 250 yards remained when Bannister blew past Chataway and sprinted wildly toward the tape. He collapsed upon crossing the finish line and heard his time officially announced only as "three minutes and…" before being mobbed. It was a funny contradiction—in a pursuit where a split-second would differentiate fame from failure, the only thing that mattered to the ears was the number of minutes.

While Bannister's fame has remained for more than a half-century (in 1975, he was knighted by Queen Elizabeth II), his record stood for less than two months before Landy broke it…with much less hoopla. It has since been shattered numerous times and, with the benefit of faster tracks and better footwear, several more seconds have been shaved off the four-minute mile. As of 2007 the record-holder was Moroccan Hicham El Guerrouj, who ran a 3:43.13 in Rome in 1999. (The women's mark is owned by Russia's Svetlana Masterkova, who in 1996 was clocked at 4:12.56 in Zurich.)

Bannister retired from competitive running at the end of 1954 to focus full-time on medical school; he later became a consultant neurologist. Yet, as the 50th anniversary of his achievement approached, he remained as determined as he was that day in Oxford, saying, "It may seem incredible now that the world record at this classic distance could be set by an amateur athlete, in bad weather, on a university running track. This is why I hope that this serves as an inspiration to sportsmen and women everywhere to keep striving to achieve their best through personal effort alone."

LIVING UP TO THE HYPE—**THIS TIME**

Mark Spitz

At the 1968 Olympics in Mexico City, U.S. swimmer Mark Spitz won two gold medals, a silver, and a bronze. Normally, this would be cause for celebration. The only problem was that the brazen 18-year-old, with 10 world record times already to his credit, had gone public predicting that he would take home six gold medals from those Games. When high altitude met high attitude, Spitz more or less belly flopped.

But four years later he proved beyond a shadow of a doubt that you can swim quite well with your tail between your legs. At Munich in 1972 (shortly before tragedy struck in the form of the terrorist hostage crisis), Mark Spitz rose up and redeemed himself, becoming the first athlete in history to win seven gold medals at a single Olympiad.

The reigning Sullivan Award winner as the nation's top amateur athlete, Spitz more than made up for the sting of the '68 Games, where both of his golds came as part of relay teams. At Munich he swam in seven events over eight days, and not only did he go undefeated, both individually and as a team member, but Spitz set or helped set a world record in every single event he participated in.

That is what's called operating at the top of your game. First up for the Indiana University graduate was swimming's most difficult stroke—and his favorite—the 200-meter butterfly. Just 2:00.7 later, he had tasted his first solo gold.

After that, the precious medals came fast and furious, prompting *Time* magazine to call him "America's secret weapon for reversing the gold flow." The results, for those of you keeping score at home:

- 200-meter freestyle (1:52.78)
- 100-meter butterfly (54.27)
- 100-meter freestyle (51.22)
- 4 x 100-meter freestyle relay (3:26.42)
- 4 x 200-meter freestyle relay (7:35.78)
- 4 x 100-meter medley relay (3:48.16)

The 100-meter freestyle was the most difficult event with the greatest chance of slippage for Spitz—even though he held the world record, there were many top sprinters in the field gunning for him.

"If I never swam the 100 free, which was the sprint event, then I wouldn't have been recognized at the fastest swimmer in the world," Spitz said 30 years after the fact, sharing that his favorite memory of the '72 Games was finishing that race. He led from the start and never faltered, shaving .25 seconds off his world record time by beating U.S. teammate Jerry Heidenreich in 51.22 seconds.

Although his youthful boasts in '68 may have made him seem cocky, Spitz actually understood that there was a large psychological component to his sport.

"Part of winning is the phenomena of being able to convince those that compete against you that they are competing for second," said the 52-year-old Spitz. "If you are a golfer today, every time you go out there and Tiger Woods was in the field of play, you wouldn't be thinking about beating him, you'd be thinking about whom amongst us is going to get second."

In 1972, that's what Mark Spitz had the whole world thinking, with a gold bonanza that may never be matched.

11th HEAVEN

Mark Spitz's final Olympic medal count totaled 11 (nine gold, one silver, one bronze), a number equaled by only two other American athletes:
  Matt Biondi (swimming)
  Carl Osburn (shooting)

STROKES OF GENIUS Mark Spitz is hoisted by helpful relay teammates after winning his unprecedented seventh gold medal at the 1972 Munich Olympics.

10.0

THE **PERFECT** TONIC FOR THE **IM**PERFECT GAMES

Nadia Comaneci

In the 1976 Olympics, Romanian gymnast Nadia Comaneci was a perfect 1.00.

That's not a typo.

Of course, history shows that Comaneci's unprecedented marks in the Montreal Games were seven separate perfect scores of 10.0. However, because the authorities in the sport had never even contemplated an athlete attaining that level of excellence, the electronic scoreboards were capable only of flashing a maximum score of 9.99. Thus, flabbergasted officials on the site had to scramble for a temporary solution and slide a decimal over when her Day 1 uneven bars performance was complete.

A 14-year-old, 4'11½", 86-pound pixie blessed with uncommon strength, grace, and agility, Comaneci (pronounced coe-muh-NETCH) had accomplished the unthinkable and set the sporting world on its ear. Part of the reason was that she was unusually lacking in another important category.

"She has no fear," said her admiring coach, Bela Karolyi.

It was July 18, 1976, and already Comaneci was the buzz of the whole Olympics. Talk about a great way to psyche out your competition. Not that Comaneci seemed to worry about the other gymnasts—or even failure.

"She has a fantastic mind," said Rod Hill, head manager of the U.S. Olympic women's team. "She can block out the whole world. It's just her and the apparatus."

For Comaneci, the apparatus of choice was the uneven bars, and she attacked it with such ferocious virtuosity that there was no other choice but to award her the first perfect score in Olympic history.

Little Nadia, although not exactly boastful, wasn't entirely bowled over by the developments. "It is really nothing new," she said at the time. On a personal level, she was speaking the truth, having achieved the perfect score in up to 20 meets during the preceding year.

NOBODY LIKE NADIA Fourteen-year-old Romanian gymnast Nadia Comaneci achieved perfection at the 1976 Montreal Olympics, with the first-ever scores of 10.0.

Her technique was flawless, her physical endurance peerless. Hill reported witnessing a practice session where Comaneci performed six consecutive 20-second routines on the uneven bars, "and wasn't even breathing hard or missing a move on the sixth one."

Because her dominance was so overwhelming, there was some initial backlash. "She's no 14-year-old girl; she's a machine, really," opined one British radio commentator. Perhaps it was because she was from an Eastern Bloc country competing in North America in the midst of the Cold War, and perhaps it was in part because she'd stoically said, "I never smile," during an earlier U.S. tour. But in the end, her charming personality shone through just as champion Olga Korbut's had four years earlier. Nadia-mania gripped the Games and the world.

Newsweek summed up the Comaneci effect: "Amid the political feuds, cheating scandals, and impromptu squabbles that have become semi-official Olympic events, Nadia in flight was Montreal's doll-like symbol of what's still right with the Games."

Once she had put that first perfect score up, tickets for the rest of the gymnastics events became scarce. To see Comaneci, people were spending $200 to buy $16 tickets. Six more perfect 10s were in the offing, as Comaneci continued to rule the uneven bars and also achieved the ultimate score on the beam. Teammates and opponents alike all agreed—Nadia was truly performing at another level.

Overall, she took home three gold medals for the uneven bars, the beam, and the all-around title, becoming the youngest ever all-around champion in Olympic history. And because of a rule change requiring entrants to turn 16 in the same calendar year as the Games to be eligible, she will always be the youngest champion.

That seems only fitting, since Nadia Comaneci truly one-upped the world. 1.0 or 10.0, her perfection will last forever.

Roger Clemens

April 29, 1986, was a damp and chilly evening, and Boston's Boys of Summer, the Red Sox, were far from the top of the sporting public's mind.

Sure, the team had its share of stars—among them Wade Boggs, Jim Rice, Dwight Evans, and a 23-year-old hard-throwing righty named Roger Clemens, who would be making the start that night at Fenway Park against the woebegone Seattle Mariners. And though competitive each season, the Sox hadn't sniffed the playoffs since their 1978 collapse to Bucky Dent and the New York Yankees. Moreover, the 9-8 mark they carried into the game was hardly telling of the magic and heartbreak that would befall the team months later in the AL playoffs and World Series. The Mariners, meanwhile, were anything but competitive as they embarked on a 67-95 campaign, their 10th straight losing season since joining the American League in 1977. They provided perfect fodder for Clemens, making his fourth start since off-season shoulder surgery.

With good reason, most of the city's sports fans channeled their attention to the NBA and the Boston Celtics' second-round playoff contest against the Atlanta Hawks, taking place at Boston Garden, as the team worked its way to a 16th world championship. Any remaining attention was being given to the defending AFC champion New England Patriots, who earlier that day had introduced their first-round pick, Southern Methodist University running back Reggie Dupard, to the local media.

Clemens had shown flashes of dominance in his first two years with the Red Sox, having won 16 games while striking out 200 batters in $231\frac{2}{3}$ innings. And he won his first three starts of 1986, beating the White Sox, the defending World Series champion Royals, and the Tigers. But 20 strikeouts? In one game? It was a magical figure that had eluded the game's greatest fireballers—Johnson, Feller, Koufax, Carlton, and Ryan. What would make this kid—as good as he was—any different?

As a crowd of 13,414—barely one-third of Fenway Park's capacity—was settling into its seats, Clemens started the game by striking out the side, with Spike Owen, Phil Bradley, and Ken Phelps all going down swinging. He added two more K's in the second, and the march toward history was in full swing (or should that be full swing and a miss?). Clemens set down at least one batter in every inning and at one point struck out eight straight Mariners, matching an AL record. More amazingly, he didn't issue a single walk in the game.

Only a seventh-inning solo home run by designated hitter Gorman Thomas, which actually gave the Mariners a brief 1-0 lead, spoiled Clemens's shutout bid. The Sox finally got to Seattle starter Mike Moore in the bottom of that inning when Evans swatted a two-out, three-run blast. In the ninth, Owen—who later in the season would be dealt to the Sox—became Clemens's 19th strikeout victim. Bradley, fanning for the fourth time, was the record-breaking number 20. Phelps at least had a moral victory in his last at-bat, grounding out to short to end the game.

Manager John McNamara observed afterward, "I watched perfect games by Catfish Hunter and Mike Witt, but this was the most awesome pitching performance I've ever seen."

ROCKET MAN Roger Clemens looks skyward after his 20th strikeout against the Detroit Tigers in 1996. Ten years earlier, he established the Major League record by striking out 20 Seattle Mariners.

29'2 1/2"

The Man Who Could Fly

The 1968 Mexico City Olympics generated plenty of controversy, most notably due to the black-gloved civil rights protest of U.S. sprinters Tommie Smith and John Carlos. But it also left the apolitical, inspirational legacy of a gargantuan leap by U.S. long jumper Bob Beamon.

In track-and-field events, where new records are usually coaxed into existence by virtue of mere decimals on the stopwatch or scant millimeters on the tape, Beamon's feat was a radical shift in the time-space continuum.

Consider if you will that before Beamon's historic leap, no long jumper had even approached 28 feet in competition, let alone 29.

"COMPARED TO THIS JUMP, WE ARE AS CHILDREN."

—Igor Ter-Ovanesyan,
USSR Olympic long jumper

Igor Ter-Ovanesyan and Beamon's Olympic teammate, Ralph Boston, jointly held the previous existing mark of 27 feet, 4¾ inches. But in a matter of seconds, the lanky 22-year-old 6'3" native of Jamaica, New York, made a breathtaking, great leap forward.

Beamon entered the Olympic Games having won the long-jump competition in 22 of his previous 23 meets, including the National AAU and the Olympic trials. The schoolboy triple-jump record-holder was an up-and-coming star and considered a good bet for the gold. However, nobody was expecting the sublime.

Competing before 45,000 roaring fans, with a civil rights protest in his recent past and dealing with the knowledge that Smith and Carlos had already been expelled from the Olympics in response to their actions, Beamon was unflappable.

"When I went to the top of the runway to begin the approach for my jump (his very first attempt of the Games), my frame of mind was awesome," Beamon told *The New York Times* years later in an interview. "I was positively motivated and disciplined; I was existing somewhere between time and space. I heard the cheering and the roars a while and then no sounds at all, only an inner voice telling me to heighten that thing within myself that had been acquired from all the training and practice. The effort had to be natural and perfect."

It was.

Beamon propelled himself so high and far that he nearly cleared the pit and overshot the new electronic recording equipment that had been installed for the Games. While the crowd buzzed excitedly, Beamon wandered around, almost as if in a daze. When the international judges put up the metric measurement first, 8.90 meters, Boston told Beamon that he thought he'd cleared 29 feet.

"What happened to 28?" Beamon asked.

When he was officially informed of his monumental distance, Beamon sank to his knees.

The following year, Beamon repeated as National AAU champion but competed sporadically after that. His record stood for a generation—it was 23 years before fellow American Mike Powell surpassed Beamon, and even that was just by a couple inches, at 29'4½". He was elected to the Olympic Hall of Fame in 1983. With his wife, Milana Walter Beamon, he is co-author of his autobiography, fittingly titled *The Man Who Could Fly.*

GREAT LEAP FORWARD U.S. long jumper Bob Beamon sails toward the gold medal and a world record at the 1968 Mexico City Olympics.

59

Al Geiberger

AT THE 1977 MEMPHIS CLASSIC, AL GEIBERGER TARGETED GOLF'S PRIME NUMBER.

As anyone who has ever picked up a set of clubs can attest, perfection is an impossible pursuit in the game of golf. But on a steamy afternoon on June 10, 1977, Al Geiberger came as close as we've ever seen.

The 39-year-old Californian unloaded a 59 in the second round of the Danny Thomas Memphis Classic, an unprecedented—and still unbroken—standard on the PGA Tour.

Geiberger was hardly a flash in the pan. The Southern Cal grad owned one major title—outdueling Sam Snead for the 1966 PGA Championship at Firestone Country Club in Akron, Ohio—and had played on the United States' 1967 and 1975 Ryder Cup teams. He also staked two runner-up finishes at the U.S. Open—in 1969 when Orville Moody beat him by a stroke and again in 1976 behind Jerry Pate. In total, the lanky Geiberger—known for his habit of chomping down peanut butter sandwiches between shots to steady his nerves and

improve his stamina—collected 11 PGA Tour victories and added another 10 on the Champions (Senior) Tour. He came into Memphis winless in 1977, though he had plated titles the previous year at the Greater Greensboro Open and the Western Open.

Even before Geiberger's stunning round, that year's event had become national news when President Gerald Ford, just six months after leaving the White House, shot a hole in one during Wednesday's Pro-Am.

In the opening round of the tournament—those days played at the fashionable Colonial Country Club—Geiberger posted a 2-under-par 70. The next day he awoke to temperatures rapidly soaring toward triple digits, heat that was certain to bake the club's greens and add to the challenge of playing one of the longest tracks on the PGA circuit.

"People ask me if I thought I was going to shoot a 59," Geiberger later told *Milwaukee*

Journal Sentinel columnist Gary D'Amato. "I say, 'If I would have known that, I'd have choked to death.' It was so hot, I was just thinking about survival."

At the time, six players—none named Nicklaus—had carded rounds of 60 at a tour event. And Geiberger's first five holes give little indication he would join or, as it turned out,

"Club 59"

Entering the 2007 season, no one had eclipsed Geiberger's round in an official PGA Tour event. Chip Beck matched it at the 1991 Las Vegas Invitational, as did David Duval playing at the 1999 Bob Hope Chrysler Classic. Annika Sorenstam became the first female golfer to shoot a 59, her round coming in the 2001 Standard Register Ping Classic in Phoenix.

"Somebody could do it tomorrow," Geiberger said to D'Amato. "Half of me expects somebody to break the record any time and the other half...well, you figure there are only 18 holes, so that's 14 birdies to get to 58 on a par-72 course. You're really getting to the edge of running out of holes."

surpass this select group. Starting on the back nine with playing partners Jerry McGee and Dave Stockton, he stood at a respectable 2 under par after five holes. Then he went torrid, lining up four straight birdies to make the turn in 30, followed by a chip-in eagle on the par-5 1st hole. Suddenly he was 8 under par and the gallery was buzzing.

Two more birdies quickly followed, putting him at 10 under par. After a pair of pars, Geiberger moved within a stroke of history with birdies on the par-3 6th and par-4 7th before parring the next hole. That left the long par-4 9th, and though it was a Friday afternoon in Memphis, it had to feel like Sunday at Augusta. Calming his nerves, Geiberger nailed the drive, then lofted a perfect 9-iron shot that left his ball 10 feet from the cup. Known to use a penny as a ball mark so that President Lincoln's eyes stared directly toward the hole, this was a day that the president, the ball, and, most importantly, Geiberger possessed perfect vision. With his Ping Pal putter that had already delivered 10 birdies during the round, he sank the shot.

"Not much happened right away [when I shot 59]," he admitted to D'Amato. "It seems like the interest has just kind of grown more and more. I think when it happened, it just surprised everybody."

63 YARDS

TOM DEMPSEY'S BOOMING **KICK** LIFTED THE LOWLY SAINTS TO VICTORY.

Tom Dempsey

This may have been the ultimate "Oh, what the heck" moment.

It was November 8, 1970, and the New Orleans Saints, going nowhere in their fourth NFL season, trailed the playoff-bound Detroit Lions, 17-16, with two seconds remaining. There they were on their own 45-yard line, and head coach J.D. Roberts—who only days earlier had replaced the fired Tom Fears—was faced with two bad options: have quarterback Billy Kilmer sling a prayer of a pass downfield in hopes of a touchdown (or defensive penalty) or ask 23-year-old kicker Tom Dempsey to—get this—attempt a 63-yard field goal.

The kick would be seven yards longer than the NFL record, set 17 years earlier by the Colts' Bert Rechichar. After being assured by Dempsey that he could make it, Roberts responded, "Go kick it."

Dempsey had already hit three field goals that day, and New Orleans was in the lead until Errol Mann booted an 18-yard field goal with 11 seconds remaining in the game. That seemed like it would be enough for the Lions, who would finish

10-4 and earn a Wild Card bid out of the old NFC Central Division. But after the kickoff, Kilmer connected with Al Dodd for a 17-yard gain that put the ball near midfield and stopped the clock.

What remained of the crowd of 66,000 buzzed in anticipation, but as Dempsey lined up the kick behind long-snapper Jackie Burkett and holder Joe Scarpati, he seemed far enough away to be wading in the Gulf of Mexico, not standing in Tulane Stadium. After a clean snap and perfect placement, he absolutely nailed the kick, leaving the ball to clear the crossbar by what cameras show to be at least three yards to spare. The monumental field goal gave the Saints a 19-17 triumph, though it didn't provide much momentum as it was their final victory in what turned out to be a 2-11-1 season (the other win came in week three, a 14-10 decision over the Giants).

"I knew I could kick it long enough," said Dempsey, whose primary concern was the stadium's swirling winds that frequently toyed with kickers. "I just hoped I could kick it straight enough. It seemed like it took forever to get there. I just kept watching it. Finally, the referees raised their hands that it was good."

Good? It was great, and there's more to the story. Dempsey was born with just half of his right foot—yeah, his kicking foot—and had a partially formed right hand. Still, he became a skilled defensive end at San Dieguito (California) High School and similarly starred at Palomar Junior College. It was at a college practice when Dempsey realized his gift for kicking. Using a shoe that had a flattened end and employing a straight-ahead approach that was beginning to fade from fashion (given the success of sidewinders Jan Stenerud and the Gogolak brothers), he found he could generate distance and accuracy. He signed with the Saints as a free agent in 1969 and proceeded to score a team-leading 99 points while earning a Pro Bowl invitation.

Dempsey later moved on to the Eagles, L.A. Rams, Houston Oilers, and the Bills—kicking a total of 159 field goals and scoring 729 points—before retiring after the 1979 season.

"It's Up...It's Way Up...It's Good!"

It took 28 years and nearly a mile in altitude for Dempsey's mark to finally be equaled. On October 25, 1998, the Broncos' Jason Elam, kicking at what was then Mile High Stadium in Denver, kicked a 63-yarder on the final play of the first half in a game against Jacksonville.

LONG SHOT Unlikely NFL kicker Tom Dempsey powers into a record 63-yard field goal that lifted the New Orleans Saints to a last-second victory.

THE SWEETEST THING TO COME OUT OF HERSHEY, PA, JUST MIGHT BE WHAT HAPPENED ONE NIGHT IN MARCH.

Wilt Chamberlain

He was the Babe Ruth of basketball. Other hoop superstars—Michael Jordan, Bill Russell, Magic Johnson—get lots of mention as the "best ever" in their sport, but with all due respect to Shaquille O'Neal (who once declared himself "Most Dominant Ever"), nobody has ever loomed larger in the game than Wilt Chamberlain.

Just consider some of the numbers that Wilt piled up, and this is not even including his personal life:

- 50.4 points per game scoring average in 1961-62
- Most consecutive seasons leading league in scoring (7; 1959-66)
- Most rebounds in a game (55)
- Led league in assists (1967-68), the only center ever to do so. (Average of 8.6 per game is higher than any single-season average Jordan ever put up.)

Yet however impressive those digits are, they're not what you'd think about first if you had the enviable job of compiling Wilt's résumé.

100.

Playing center for the Philadelphia Warriors, in just his third year in the NBA, Wilt was already having a spectacular season (see above scoring average). He'd already scored 40 or more points in a mind-blowing 18 consecutive games earlier in the year, and the stage was truly set on this rainy night, March 2, 1962, in Hershey, Pennsylvania. (It may seem strange, but the chocolate capital of America was where the Warriors held training camp and played a few regular-season games each year.)

It wasn't exactly Oompa-Loompas the Warriors were facing, but the Knicks were in last place, already eliminated from playoff contention, and their starting center, Phil Jordon, was out of commission with an injury. That left unproven rookie Darrall Imhoff (later an All-

Star, and involved in a trade for Chamberlain) in the pivot, going up against a Chamberlain who was champing at the bit. And just Imhoff's luck, Wilt had already proved both his luck and his accuracy earlier in the day.

Some members of the Warriors had been playing pinochle, and "Wilt was getting fantastic cards," remembers point guard Guy Rodgers. After the card game, some of the team moved on to an arcade, where Wilt proceeded to set the record for best score at the shooting gallery. "The man was just hot," Rodgers shrugged.

So it was probably no surprise that he had 23 points at the end of the first quarter, as the Warriors raced out to a big lead. Or that he added on 18 in the second quarter, giving him 41 at halftime. He was on pace to break the league record of 78 points in a game, which he himself had set earlier in the season in a triple-overtime game.

Perhaps most significantly, as a notoriously poor free throw shooter (with a career mark of just 51 percent), Wilt was on fire from the foul line. He was a perfect 8-of-8 from the stripe in the third quarter and had 69 points with 12 minutes to play.

On pace for a "mere" 92 at this point, the Big Dipper realized that he had a chance at an extremely round number, and played with even greater passion.

"We'd shoot and Wilt would take off down the court like a lonesome end," said Imhoff, who fouled out while trying to slow down the Philadelphia star. "It was like covering a receiver. It was the hardest I ever saw Wilt work."

GOT WILT? Philadelphia Warriors center Wilt Chamberlain knocks down the final basket in his outlandish 100-point explosion against the New York Knicks in 1962.

With help from his teammates (Rodgers had 20 assists) and coach Frank McGuire, who instructed players to foul the Knicks in the waning minutes in order to stop the clock, Wilt had a monstrous, 31-point fourth quarter to charter the century club. Shooting 28-of-32 from the free throw line didn't hurt, either.

He dropped in the historic hoop after frantic teammates grabbed a couple rebounds and fed him at close range with just 46 seconds left on the clock.

Even though the paid attendance was just 4,124, the place went nuts and fans stormed the court. Over the years, the legendary nature of that night has distorted people's memories.

"It's amazing, but I bet I've had 25,000 people come up to me and say they saw the game," said Chamberlain three decades afterward. "What's more amazing is, most of them say they saw it at Madison Square Garden. That's some feat. Can you imagine how good their eyes were?"

Not nearly as good as yours were, Wilt.

101: Leslie Torments Torrance

Lisa Leslie won three gold medals as a member of the U.S. Olympic women's basketball team, has won WNBA titles and MVP awards with the Los Angeles Sparks, and became the first woman to dunk in a pro basketball game.

But it was as a 6'5" senior center for Inglewood Morningside High School in Los Angeles that she made perhaps her biggest dent in the record books—she scored 101 points versus rival South Torrance. In the first half.

There was no second half, no breaking Cheryl Miller's single-game high school record of 105 points, and no run at the incomprehensible 200-point level, because the visiting South Torrance squad refused to come out of the locker room after the intermission.

Unlike Chamberlain's game, this one had some premeditation to it. Sportsmanlike or not, tradition at Morningside called for the senior captain to score as many points as possible in the last home game before the playoffs. Leslie's goal was to break the record set the year before—a paltry 68 points.

Leslie scored 49 in the first quarter and heated up in the second, scoring 52. She hit 37 of 56 shots from the floor and 27 of 35 free throws. "I was on fire," she recalls. "Runners, jumpers, everything was going in."

"The game plan was if any of my teammates got a rebound or a steal they would throw it to me," she says. "If I missed, they'd rebound and get it back to me."

They did good—except for that notorious ballhog, Sherrell Young, who scored the other point.

Philadelphia (169)

Player	Pos	Min	FG	FGA	FT	FTA	Reb	Ast	PF	Pts.
Arizin	F	31	7	18	2	2	5	4	0	16
Conlin		14	0	4	0	0	4	1	1	0
Ruklik		8	0	1	0	2	2	1	2	0
Meschery	F	40	7	12	2	2	7	3	4	16
Luckenbill		3	0	0	0	0	1	0	2	0
Chamberlain	C	48	36	63	28	32	25	2	2	100
Rodgers	G	48	1	4	9	12	7	20	5	11
Attles	G	34	8	8	1	1	5	6	4	17
Larese		14	4	5	1	1	1	2	5	9
Totals		**240**	**63**	**115**	**43**	**52**	**60**	**39**	**25**	**169**

Team Rebounds: 3

New York (147)

Player	Pos	Min	FG	FGA	FT	FTA	Reb	Ast	PF	Pts
Naulls	F	43	9	22	13	15	7	2	5	31
Green	F	21	3	7	0	0	7	1	5	6
Buckner		33	16	26	1	1	8	0	4	33
Imhoff	C	20	3	7	1	1	6	0	6	7
Budd		27	6	8	1	1	10	1	1	13
Guerin	G	46	13	29	13	17	8	6	5	39
Butler	G	32	4	13	0	0	7	3	1	8
Butcher		18	3	6	4	6	3	4	5	10
Totals		**240**	**57**	**118**	**33**	**41**	**60**	**17**	**32**	**147**

Team Rebounds: 4

Score by Quarters:

	1	2	3	4	Total
Philadelphia	42	37	46	44	169
New York	26	42	38	41	147

Wilt Chamberlain's Scoring by Quarters:

Quarter	Min	FG	FGA	FT	FTA	Reb	Ast	PF	Pts
First	12	7	14	9	9	10	0	0	23
Second	12	7	12	4	5	4	1	1	18
Third	12	10	16	8	8	6	1	0	28
Fourth	12	12	21	7	10	5	0	1	31
Totals	**48**	**36**	**63**	**28**	**32**	**25**	**2**	**2**	**100**

There are years in sports that stand out because of big numbers.

Records are made to be broken, and fans remember those special, special seasons. Sometimes the records are unthinkable and these days you just can't imagine anyone even coming close.

Back in 1961-62, the Big O, Oscar Robertson put up mind-boggling stats. Today, triple-doubles are pretty rare in the NBA. So think about this...Oscar Robertson averaged a triple-double for the entire season: 30.8 ppg, 12.5 rpg, 11.4 apg. No other NBA player has ever accomplished that feat, and I don't believe anyone else will ever come close.

He was Magic Johnson before Magic Johnson. I remember seeing him play at the University of Cincinnati, and he was remarkable. I don't know if kids today can truly appreciate what the Big O did on the hardwood.

Staying with the NBA, Michael the Magnificent, Michael Jordan, accomplished so many things in his career. One of them was leading the Bulls to a 72-10 mark, the first NBA squad to get to the 70 mark in one season. The 1971-72 Lakers with Wilt Chamberlain, Jerry West, and company got to 69, but the Bulls shattered that.

It is mind-boggling to think about 72 wins in an 82-game season. Michael was all about winning with that special mentality, and individual numbers and stats really didn't mean a thing. It was about one stat—the number of rings, baby! He got six of them, and if he didn't make the journey to face the challenge of baseball before returning to the hardwood, who knows what he

could have attained. Wow, 72 Ws on the NBA level with all of the travel, the pressure, the expectations, opponents playing at another level against you, is absolutely amazing!

In the '70s, the NFL had a couple of amazing accomplishments. The Miami Dolphins were simply perfect, going 17-0. That's right, they painted a Picasso on the gridiron, a season that has not been matched since. Members of that '72 Dolphins team celebrate each season when the last NFL unbeaten falls down to defeat!

Then in 1973, there was the Electric Company, which opened holes for O.J. Simpson. Few believed that the NFL would see a 2,000-yard rusher in one season. Simpson ran for 2,003!

Before there was a Tiger Woods, golf had an amazing performer named Byron Nelson. Think about this for a pretty good year—18 tournament wins! Most guys on the PGA Tour today would love to win that many over their entire career!

Speaking of a great year, what about 1983 and Martina Navratilova? She lost one match all year. Do you think she remembers the name Kathy Horvath? That's the same Kathy Horvath who played in the U.S. Open at age 14 in 1979! Horvath stunned Martina at the French Open for Navratilova's lone loss of the year.

You can associate a year like '61 because of the number 61. There was a movie called *61**, and Roger Maris made his mark in the history books, shattering a record that many thought would last a lifetime. Special, special, special!

Dick Vitale

IT WAS A VERY GOOD YEAR

Standout Single Season Performances

A BACKUP QUARTERBACK, A NO-NAME DEFENSE, BUT A FLAWLESS RESULT

17-0

THE 1972 MIAMI DOLPHINS

There's a moral to the Dolphins' 1972 football season. Make that a Morrall.

Because without 38-year-old quarterback Earl Morrall, the only perfect season in NFL history may never have happened. Miami was quickly becoming the class of the AFC and was the odds-on favorite to reach the Super Bowl. And with good reason: the team possessed one of the game's brightest young coaches in Don Shula, was stocked with talent on both sides of the ball (forget that "No-Name Defense" nonsense), and had advanced to Super Bowl VI a year earlier, falling to Dallas, 24-3.

The Dolphins opened the regular season with four straight victories—which included a last-minute triumph at Minnesota—and everything was right on schedule, though no one was mentioning anything about a perfect season. Why would they? Since the NFL was formed in 1920, only three teams had even managed undefeated regular seasons. The Bears did it twice—in 1934 and again in 1942—but lost in the league cham-

pionship game both times. The other team was the 1929 Packers, who minted a 12-0-1 mark back in the day before the league held playoffs.

Miami fans were more concerned with a return trip to the Super Bowl, and even those ambitions took a seemingly fatal hit in Week 5 when starting quarterback Bob Griese was brought down hard by San Diego's Ron East and suffered a broken right leg and dislocated ankle.

Warming the bench was Morrall, a former first-round draft pick of the 49ers and an on-and-off starter throughout his 17-year career. Signed in the off-season as veteran insurance, he brought a solid track record and some familiarity with Shula. In 1968 with the Colts, Morrall stepped in for an injured Johnny Unitas and was named the league's MVP while leading that Shula-coached team to Super Bowl III. In Super Bowl V, with Unitas again sidelined, he came in and lifted the Colts to victory over Dallas.

No sooner had Griese been carted off the field

BACKUP STEPS UP With Bob Griese sidelined, reserve quarterback Earl Morrall made the plays that kept the 1972 Dolphins' perfect season intact.

than defensive lineman Bill Stanfill yelled to Morrall, "Okay, old man. Get those cataracts in motion. Turn up that hearing aid and let's go."

The transition was seamless and the Dolphins rolled to a 14-0 finish, capped with their third shutout of the year, a 16-0 win over Baltimore. Morrall did exactly what was expected, completing 55.3 percent of his passes while throwing 11 touchdowns with seven interceptions. Easing his load was the backfield tandem of Larry Csonka and Mercury Morris, who became the first teammates in NFL history to rush for 1,000 yards in the same season.

Things became a bit more interesting in the playoffs. In the divisional round, Morrall needed to engineer a late 80-yard drive, capped by Jim Kiick's 8-yard touchdown run, for Miami to get past Cleveland, 20-14. Traveling to Pittsburgh for the AFC Championship Game (in those days hosting the title game was rotated and not based on record), the Dolphins found themselves locked in a 7-7 tie at halftime. That's when Shula inserted a now-healthy Griese back into the lineup, who proceeded to direct scoring drives of 80 and 49 yards, both capped by Kiick touchdown jaunts. Linebacker Nick Buoniconti sealed the 21-17 win by intercepting the Steelers' Terry Bradshaw at midfield.

Despite all their achievements—they led the NFL in nearly every offensive and defensive category—the Dolphins entered Super Bowl VII as a field-goal underdog to the George Allen–coached Washington Redskins. But Washington's fate was the same as Miami's first 16 opponents: defeat.

Two first-half touchdowns—on Griese's 28-yard hookup with Howard Twilley and Kiick's

1-yard run—accounted for all the game's points until kicker Garo Yepremian walked onto the L.A. Coliseum's turf with 2:07 to play to try an insurance 42-yard field goal. Poetry was at stake: make it and the Dolphins' 17-0 season would end with a 17-0 win.

Instead, a comedy routine ensued. The Redskins' Bill Brundige blocked the kick back into Yepremian's belly. The diminutive kicker rolled right and attempted to throw an awkward pass, but his toss went backwards (it was ruled a fumble) and was caught by Washington's Mike Bass, who raced 49 yards for a touchdown. That made the score a slightly more uncomfortable 14-7.

"If we lose this game, I'll kill you," snarled Dolphins safety Jake Scott to the embarrassed kicker.

Miami won—Washington's final play ended with a sack by Stanfill on quarterback Bill Kilmer—and Yepremian lived.

Wait a Minute

The 1972 Dolphins weren't completely perfect. They lost three preseason games that year, falling to Detroit, Green Bay, and Washington. Their official win streak reached 18 games before losing to Oakland, 12-7, in Week 2 of the 1973 season. They finished the '73 season at 12-2 (the other blemish being a 16-3 loss to Baltimore), then rolled through the playoffs with wins over Cincinnati, Oakland, and, finally, the Vikings in Super Bowl VIII. "That team was better than the one in '72," insists Wayne Huizenga, now the Dolphins' owner, but then a season-ticket holder.

That team's legacy still lives on. In 1985, Chicago won its first 12 games before losing on *Monday Night Football* to, drum roll please, the Miami Dolphins. The 1998 Broncos and 2005 Colts both started out 13-0 before being beaten.

And while arguments have raged for decades about where the '72 Dolphins rank in the history of the NFL's best teams, Csonka summed it up best: "Perfection ends a lot of arguments."

MIAMI DOLPHINS' Jim Mandich takes in a Bob Griese pass during Super Bowl VII against the Washington Redskins.

18

MOST GOLFERS **PLAY 18.**
IN 1945, HE **WON 18.**

Byron Nelson

Leo Durocher was wrong: nice guys don't finish last. At least not in the case of Byron Nelson, who was universally acclaimed as one of the finest gentlemen ever to play the game of golf.

It was quite the converse in 1945, when the gracious Texan known as "Lord Byron" won a whopping 18 tournaments on the PGA Tour, including an incomprehensible 11 consecutive events.

This lean, 6'1" rancher with massive hands possessed a long, fluid stroke that was considered by many experts to be the ideal way to strike the ball. So much so that the machine used by the USGA (United States Golf Association) in the 1960s for testing golf balls and clubs was dubbed the "Iron Byron." And if his swing was bulletproof, so too are his records.

The next highest single-season win totals are 13 by Ben Hogan and 11 by Sam Snead, and Tiger Woods has the second-best streak, with seven consecutive tournament victories.

"In this day and age, with this competition, to win 11 in a row would be almost unheard of," Woods told the Associated Press. "What Byron accomplished, that goes down as one of the great years in the history of our sport.... Joe DiMaggio's record, I see that being broken more than winning 11 in a row."

Of course, 1945 marked the last year of World War II, and the PGA tour was actually suspended for two months that year in consideration of the events of the day. The only "major" tournament held was the PGA, which Nelson won.

But even under those wartime circumstances, the 33-year-old Nelson still had to face the likes of Snead and Hogan that year and was quite simply playing the best golf in the history of the sport. To anyone who knows the fickle nature of golf, the numbers that Nelson put up over a three-year period almost do not compute: in 75 starts from 1944 to the end of 1946, he won 34 times and finished second 16 times. In those three years, he finished out of the top 10 just once, and it was the 1945 season that really cemented his legend.

With 18 victories, seven second-place finishes, 19 consecutive rounds under 70, and a scoring average of 68.33 (including 67.45 in the fourth round—not even wearing red, Tiger), Nelson was simply incendiary.

He won every which way. The second win of his streak concluded with a memorable playoff against Snead at the Charlotte Open. At the Tam O'Shanter in Chicago, he decimated the field, with runner-up Hogan needing binoculars, finishing 11 strokes behind. At the Seattle Open, he carded a then-record 62 for 18 holes and a world-record 259 for 72 holes, 29 shots under par. He even won a two-ball tournament, a format no longer used on the pro circuit.

"When I was playing regularly, I had a goal," Nelson recalled years later. "I could see the prize money going into the ranch, buying a tractor, or a cow. It gave me incentive."

Then, at the top of his game—with two Masters, two PGA's and a U.S. Open among his 52 titles—Nelson retired from full-time competition at 34, just two years after his magnificent 1945 season. He continued a lifelong association with the sport he loved until his death at age 94, serving as a commentator and mentor to the younger generations, including luminaries such as Ken Venturi and Tom Watson. In 2006 he was posthumously awarded the Congressional Gold Medal.

Even for the legends of the game, Nelson is legendary. Arnold Palmer, who grew up idolizing the man, said, "Byron Nelson accomplished things on the pro tour that never have been and never will be approached."

"If he had kept playing like guys do now," said Woods, "more than likely he would have won more [career] tournaments than anyone."

In the year 2000, the humble Nelson reflected back on the year he won more often than anybody could imagine: "Anytime you make a record stand for 55 years, why, you've done pretty good," he said.

IN 1961-62, OSCAR ROBERTSON
BECAME BASKETBALL'S MOST
LETHAL TRIPLE THREAT.

30.8 PPG
12.5 RPG
11.4 APG

The Big "O"

It's poetic, really. O. Leave it to a guy nicknamed "The Big O" to be the most well-rounded player that pro basketball has ever seen. Listen up, youngsters: before there was a Magic Johnson or Larry Bird or LeBron James, there was Oscar Robertson.

Born in 1938, Robertson grew up in a poverty-stricken housing project in Indianapolis, where he first learned the game that he loved by shooting tennis balls wrapped with rags into a peach basket. Flash forward to the Big O as a young man who had already won two state championships at Crispus Attucks High School in Indiana.

Shattering prototypes as a 6'5", 210-pound point guard, Robertson then elevated the University of Cincinnati's program to national prominence with three scoring titles and two Final Four appearances. After graduation, he co-captained (with Jerry West) the 1960 U.S Olympic team to golden heights, making that next step—to the pro level—not that tough of a transition. Clearly.

After finishing third in the league in scoring with over 30 points per game for the Cincinnati Royals, he was honored as both the NBA's Rookie of the Year and All-Star Game MVP, but the Big O had lots more in store for 1961-62.

Actually, it was less like a store, and more like a supermarket. Check out this inventory: 30.8 points per game; 12.5 rebounds per game; and 11.4 assists per game. Today's players gain headlines when they achieve such a "triple double" (double-digit totals in three of the major statistical categories) in a single game. The Big O averaged that level of production for an entire season, the only NBA player ever to do so. Want something even better? Robertson's stats for the first five years of his career averaged out to a triple double, at 30.3 points, 10.4 rebounds, and 10.6 assists per game.

He could shoot, he could drive, he could pass, and he could rebound. He did all of those things with both passion and methodical intensity, adapting his game to exploit his opponent's weaknesses.

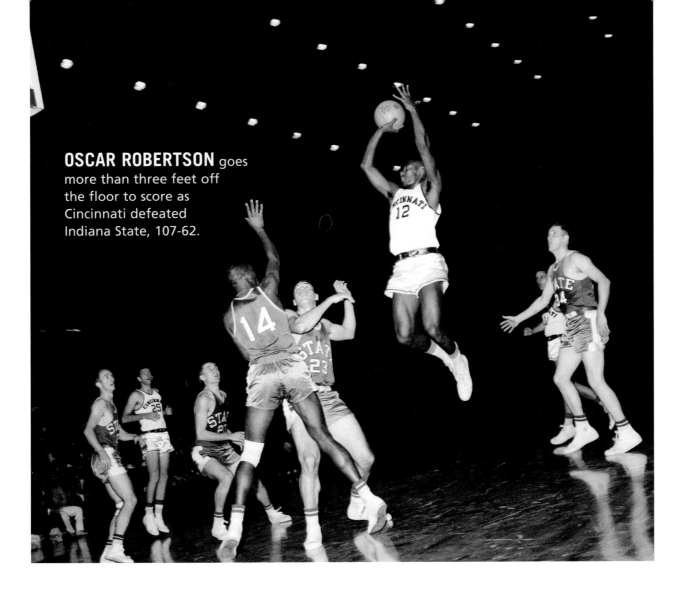

OSCAR ROBERTSON goes more than three feet off the floor to score as Cincinnati defeated Indiana State, 107-62.

"My game was just to go out and start playing," Robertson said. "If you play hard enough, you're going to get your shots, you're going to get your rebounds, and you're going to get your assists. I never put an emphasis on one area of the game, but to play successfully and win, you have to do two things—rebound and play defense. That hasn't changed throughout the history of the game."

Another thing that hasn't changed is the enormous difficulty in attaining a triple double. The top modern achiever in that realm, New Jersey Nets All-Star guard Jason Kidd, had 87 in his career at the end of the 2006-07 season, 94 behind Robertson's career total of 181. Kidd knows full well the obstacles inherent in the chase for triple doubles.

"Everything has to go your way," Kidd says. "Your teammates have to knock down shots, you have to knock down shots, and then you have to go battle with the trees—the big guys—for rebounds. Sometimes people think it's easier than it is. Everything has to go your way that night, and so for Oscar to average one for a whole season is just unbelievable."

But that's exactly what Robertson specialized in—the unbelievable.

49

IN 2004, THE COLTS' QUARTERBACK WAS PACKING A GOLDEN TOUCHDOWN GUN.

Peyton Manning

If the NFL's accountants are on the ball, they really should send an invoice for expenses incurred in the year 2004 to Peyton Manning.

As quarterback and leader of the Indianapolis Colts' offensive juggernaut, Manning's exploits forced stadiums around the league to blow their maintenance budgets, replacing burned-out scoreboard lights and first-down chains abused to the point of elasticity. Likewise, play-by-play announcers purchased record quantities of lozenges, their throats raw from calling Manning's myriad scoring drives. Antacid sales also went through the roof—the primary market being queasy defenses forced by cruel schedule-makers to face him.

Okay, so maybe the Dow Jones can't verify all the above assertions, but one thing is certain—Manning was money, shredding secondaries and sections of the NFL record book by throwing 49 touchdown passes during a magical regular season.

Entering his seventh campaign, the top pick of the 1998 draft and son of former Saints quar-terback Archie Manning already had a spectacular career in progress: a co-MVP season the year before (shared with Tennessee quarterback Steve McNair), four Pro Bowl appearances, nearly 25,000 passing yards, and 167 touchdown passes.

But nobody was prepared for the season-long clinic Manning conducted in 2004, when he eclipsed Dan Marino's seemingly untouchable record of 48 touchdown passes...with a game to spare.

"Well, I'd like to thank [Peyton] for making me an offensive genius," laughed head coach Tony Dungy, known primarily for his defensive acumen in his previous gig at Tampa Bay.

One of every three Colts possessions ended with a Manning touchdown pass, and one out of every 10 passes he threw resulted in a touchdown. Compare that to his interceptions—just one out of every 50 throws. Even the most bearish of economists would take note of that bottom line. Manning also matched a league record by tossing multiple touchdown passes in each of the season's first 13 games, and shattered another one by throwing four touchdowns or more in five consecutive games.

Perhaps the scariest statistic of the year might have been this—2004 marked the first season in which Manning attempted fewer than 500 passes (497, to be exact). All that from the league's only quarterback to call his own plays. Manning's Colts finished with a 12-4 record, won their second straight AFC South crown, and scored an astounding 522 points, the most in the league. They tallied more points in the first half of each of their games (277) than seven NFL teams managed the entire year.

"Playing against him is like a chess match," said Troy Polamalu, the All-Pro safety from the archrival Pittsburgh Steelers.

Of course it didn't hurt that he could deploy pieces like perennial favorite Marvin Harrison, the All-Pro who melded with Peyton into the most prolific quarterback-wide receiver duo in league history (by the end of 2006, they held NFL records for most completions, passing yards, and touchdowns together). Harrison latched onto 15 scoring passes (14 from Peyton) and was also joined in double figures by a couple of young pawns who burst into bishop-dom, Reggie Wayne (12 touchdowns, 11 from Manning) and Brandon Stokley (10 touchdowns).

Stokley caught the record-breaker, and it came with just 56 seconds left in regulation as the 11-3 Colts came back to beat the playoff-bound San Diego Chargers in overtime.

"The way it happened on that drive, I think Johnny Unitas would have been proud," said Manning, alluding to another Colts legend.

That may be true, Peyton, but Johnny's estate ain't coughing up for the 49 celebratory-spike-damaged footballs.

OUTMANNING THE DEFENSE Colts quarterback Peyton Manning torched foes throughout the 2004 NFL season with a record-setting 49 touchdown passes.

50 in 39

The Great One!

Leave it to a loving father to put a budding legend in his place. When young Wayne Gretzky, then 20 years old and a third-year center for the Edmonton Oilers in 1981-82, phoned home to tell his folks that he'd just pulverized Maurice "Rocket" Richard and Mike Bossy's record for scoring 50 goals in the fewest number of games (they each did it in 50), his dear dad Walter responded with, "What took you so long?"

Of course, he was just teasing, but Wayne's mom and dad probably were mildly disappointed, as they'd planned to fly to Edmonton that coming week in hopes of seeing their son break said record.

You see, after playing 37 games, Wayne had a total of 41 goals to his credit and was on a pretty solid pace to break the benchmark. But that season, the elder Gretzkys relearned the same lesson the entire NHL was being taught—when Greatness calls, you cannot stop it.

In a sport where scoring three goals in one game earns you headlines and inspires the crowd to fling their chapeaus iceward, Gretzky fired in four goals against the Los Angeles Kings in Game 38, hiking his total up to 45. Then, in the very next game, in front of a roaring home crowd at Northlands Coliseum, he tallied five goals against the Philadelphia Flyers to ratchet up his season total to 50, all in a breathtaking 39 games.

The last tally was an empty-netter with :03 left on the clock, after the Flyers had pulled goalie Pete Peeters in a last-ditch effort to tie it up. The historic goal iced the Oilers' 7-5 victory.

And Mom and Dad didn't even hear the game on the radio.

"Never in my wildest imagination did I expect to score five goals against a tough team like the Flyers, but it was one of those games where everything went my way," offered the typically understated Gretzky.

He's too modest. More like one of those careers, really. The Great One went on to smash idol Gordie Howe's all-time NHL scoring record, finishing up with an incredible 2,857 points, including 894 goals.

At an even six feet tall and a slender 180 pounds, Gretzky did not loom large over the ice, and his skating speed was good but not exceptional. However, he'd been a phenom since he was a youngster, a six-year-old star skating in a league full of 10- and 12-year-olds, seemingly preternaturally disposed to following his father's brilliant advice—"skate to where the puck is going, not to where it has been."

The result was so magical, even his foes couldn't help but praise him. Feisty veteran Bobby Clarke, Philadelphia's three-time Hart Trophy winner, was on the ice that historical night and threw around a gigantic name by way of comparison.

"At least with Bobby Orr, you'd see him wind up in his own end and you could try to set up some kind of defense to stop him," said Clarke. "Gretzky just comes out of nowhere...it's scary."

Even old-timers whose records had been obliterated were obliged to acknowledge Gretzky's unique gift. "There's no doubt he would have scored—maybe not as many goals—in my day," said Richard. "But he would have been the best scorer in the league."

By the time he played his 50th game that season, Gretzky had already piled up 61 goals. Phil

Esposito's single-season record of 76 fell a few weeks later, and the Great One wound up finishing his relentless, 80-game lamp-lighting campaign with a staggering 92 goals. Scarier still, the habitually unselfish Gretzky had even more assists, becoming the first-ever NHL player to cross the 200-point threshold in one season, with 212 total points.

"He's like a phantom," added Philly defenseman Behn Wilson. "You think you've got him lined up in your sights and all of the sudden he's behind you."

Or, more accurately, just out of reach. Just like his records.

(photo courtesy Getty Images)

OVER THE COURSE OF A HALF-CENTURY, A SLUGGER WENT FROM REVILED TO REVERED.

Roger Maris

When Roger Maris slugged 61 home runs for the Yankees in 1961, his accomplishment was welcomed with all the enthusiasm of a colonoscopy. While in his pursuit of history, the reticent right fielder found himself thrust into an unwanted competition that included teammate Mickey Mantle, the legendary Babe Ruth, and New York's bloodthirsty media. Even Commissioner Ford Frick piled on. And once Maris broke the mark—on the season's final day—it was lassoed with a "Yeah, but" tag that stuck for the next 30 years.

Maris had been a multi-sport athlete at Shanley High School in Fargo, North Dakota, who once ran back four kickoffs for touchdowns in a single game, yet passed up a football scholarship at the University of Oklahoma to sign a contract with baseball's Cleveland Indians. He reached the major leagues in 1957 at the age of 23 and the following season was dealt to the Kansas City Athletics. It was there that he caught the eyes of scouts who thought his text-book lefty swing would serve him well at Yankee Stadium. After an all-star 1959 campaign, he was the principal part of a seven-player trade that sent him to New York.

Anyone who maintains that Maris was a single-year sensation must not know what he did in 1960. Midway through his debut campaign with the Yanks, he had 27 home runs and 60 RBIs and, despite missing 17 games later in the year, was chosen the American League's Most Valuable Player. He topped the circuit in RBIs, extra base hits, and slugging percentage, and his 39 homers ranked second in the league, one behind teammate Mantle.

The controversy that followed was mostly beyond Maris's control. Before the start of the 1961 season, the American League expanded to 10 teams, adding the Los Angeles Angels and Minnesota Twins, and created a 162-game schedule where teams played each other 18 times. (The eight-team National League stayed at 154 games until the Mets and Houston Colt

ROGER THAT The Yankees' Roger Maris launches his record-breaking 61st home run on the final day of the 1961 season.

.45s were added in 1962.)

Although Maris didn't connect on his first-round tripper until Game 11, he soon caught fire, drilling 11 home runs in May and 15 more in June. By the end of August, he had 51. He and Mantle went toe-to-toe in the home run race for most of the season—with fans, media, and even the Yankee front office rooting for "the Mick"—and both were poised to shatter Ruth's record of 60 home runs until a leg injury sidelined the Yankee centerfielder.

Yet if opposing pitchers couldn't stop Maris, then Commissioner Frick could. He rationalized that since Ruth accomplished his mark in 154 games, baseball would recognize both home run records if Maris needed more games do it. In Game 154 at Baltimore, Maris homered once and just missed a second, putting him at 59. He swatted number 60 on September 26, in the team's 159th game, then broke the record in the regular-season finale—a 1-0 win over the Red Sox—by sending a fourth-inning Tracy Stallard fastball over the right field fence. Less than 24,000 fans were on hand at Yankee Stadium to witness it.

Maris was again named AL Most Valuable Player. And although he batted just .105 in the World Series against the Reds, one of his hits was a ninth-inning home run to win Game 3. The Yankees took the series in five.

Despite injuries and the game's movement toward power pitching, Maris continued to hit well. He totaled 33 home runs and 100 RBIs in 1962, when the Yankees again won the World Series, and had 23 round-trippers the next sea-son despite being limited to 90 games. He moved on to St. Louis in 1967, helping the Cardinals to the World Series title that year by hitting .385 and knocking in seven runs in their seven-game triumph over the Red Sox. Maris retired following the 1968 season, with 275 career home runs and a .260 lifetime average.

No one argues that he was bitter upon leaving the game, muttering, "It would have been a helluva lot more fun if I had not hit those 61 home runs." One popular myth is that Maris's hair fell out in clumps during his pursuit of Ruth.

Fast-forward to the late 1990s and the mega-muscled (and possibly chemically enriched) Sammy Sosa, Mark McGwire, and Barry Bonds, who all sailed by Maris's record. Sosa topped out at 66 home runs; McGwire hit 70; and Bonds belted 73 out of the park in 2001. But once fans took a second look at their bodies and what was once suspected became shamefully accepted, Maris suddenly re-emerged as the standard-bearer for all that was right with the game.

By then, Commissioner Fay Vincent had removed Maris's "dual listing" with Ruth. In 2001 came the HBO movie *61**, directed by Billy Crystal, which painted a sympathetic portrait of Maris. A website was established asking one million fans to sign a petition calling on Major League Baseball to return the home run record to him. And in 2005 the North Dakota Senate unanimously approved a resolution requesting Maris be reinstated as baseball's single-season home run leader.

Too bad Maris wasn't around to see any of it. He might have finally had the satisfaction he was never able to enjoy during or after his historic season. He passed away on December 14, 1985, at the age of 51, losing a two-year battle with lymphoma cancer. At least he did live to see his No. 9 retired by the Yankees in 1984, with New York fans finally giving him that richly deserved ovation.

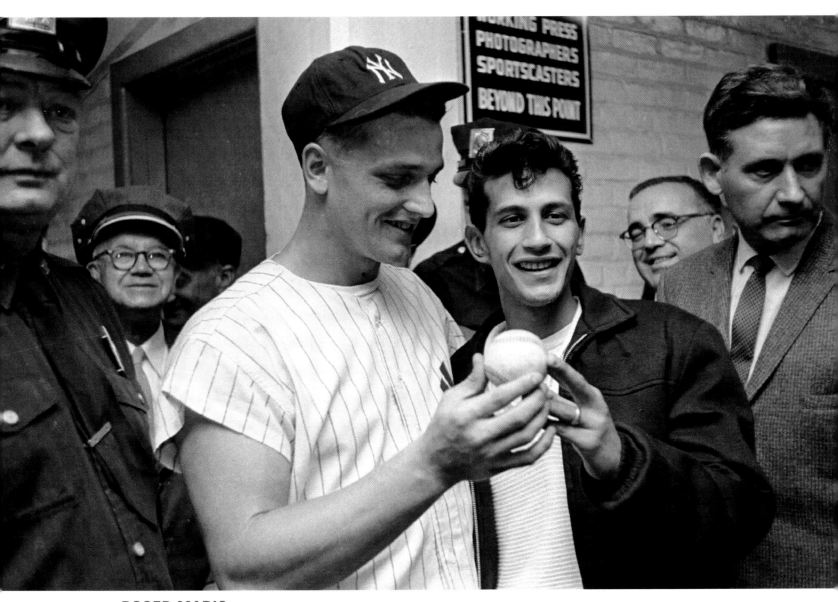

ROGER MARIS and Sal Durante. Durante caught Maris's 61st home run ball.

72-10

CHICAGO GOT ITS AIR BACK,
AND AN OLD NBA STANDARD WAS DEFLATED.

The Bulls

In 1995-96, the NBA was the Bulls' own personal Pamplona.

Before that magical season, no team in NBA history had ever reached the 70-win mark. At the time the best record in league history was the 69-13 showing of the 1971-72 Los Angeles Lakers championship team led by Jerry West and Wilt Chamberlain.

But Chicago changed all that two years after their first "three-peat" ended. With recently retired minor league outfielder Michael Jordan back in the fold, All-Star forward Scottie Pippen, freshly acquired rebounding machine Dennis Rodman, and supersub Toni Kukoc, head coach Phil Jackson's squad ran roughshod over the league on their way to a gaudy 72-10 mark that will likely stand for years to come.

"It wasn't a matter of maybe," said backup center Bill Wennington. "With Michael, Scottie, and Dennis...it didn't really matter what the other team did. We went into every game think-ing—knowing, actually—that we would win."

The Bulls started off the season by sandwich-ing two five-game win streaks around a loss at Orlando. Then they lost on the road on November 26 to Seattle, the team they would ultimately defeat in the NBA Finals.

Proving they were immune to the holiday season blues, they went undefeated from Thanks-giving to Christmas, ripping off 13 straight victories before falling on the road to a tough Indiana team on December 26. (The Reggie Miller and Rik Smits–led Pacers were the only team in the league to beat the Bulls twice in the regular season, splitting the season series.)

With their record dropping to 23-3, the annoyed Bulls then really went to work, tram-pling 18 consecutive opponents to sport a record of 41-3.

Jackson knew he had a special team on his hands when the season started, but even he said, "It's hard to translate from paper into reality as to why we're playing at the level we are."

Although the Bulls then stumbled to earth with their only losing "streak" of the season (two whole games on the road, to Denver and Phoenix), the league was officially full of believers.

They went 39-2 on their home floor (at one point holding a 44-game home court winning streak, dating to the previous season) and also established a league record with 33 wins on the road. To give you an idea of the laserlike focus and steely resolve this team had, their record for games on the weary side of back-to-back nights, the historical bane of NBA teams, was 21 wins and two losses.

They succeeded in all phases of the game. Sure, Jordan was brilliant and revitalized in his first full season back from the baseball sabbatical, winning his eighth scoring title and taking the Triple Crown of MVP trophies (All-Star Game, regular season, playoffs), but this was clearly a team effort.

The defense was domineering, allowing a stingy 92.9 points per game, as the mercurial Rodman led the league in rebounding for the fifth straight season and was joined by Jordan and Pippen on the NBA's All-Defensive first team.

BULL RUN Michael Jordan and the 1995–96 Chicago Bulls became the first NBA team to crack the 70-win barrier and then went on to beat the SuperSonics for the league championship.

Jackson and assistant coach Tex Winter's fluid "triangle" offense was run to perfection, with Jordan surrounded by deadly sidemen Pippen and Kukoc and savvy role players like center Luc Longley, Ron Harper, and Steve Kerr, who ranked second in the NBA in three-point shooting percentage.

The Bulls kept up the pace down the homestretch, simultaneously reaching the 70-win mark and passing the old-school Lakers in the 79th game of the season by holding off the Milwaukee Bucks, 86-80.

86-1

Martina Navratilova

The answer to the obvious question is Kathy Horvath.

The obvious question is who was the lone player to defeat Martina Navratilova in 1983?

Navratilova, the overpowering lefty who made center court a second home throughout her illustrious career, finished the year 86-1 (for a .989 winning percentage), captured 16 of the 17 tournaments she entered, and earned nearly $1.5 million. The tennis world had never seen anything like it.

Not that Navratilova's 1982 was all that bad, when she posted a 90-3 match record, or her 1984, when she went 78-2 and earned more money than any athlete outside of professional boxing. Or her 1985, '86, and '87, when she played her way into the final of every major, capped by the ultra-rare singles-doubles-mixed-doubles trifecta at the US Open.

But 1983 stands alone on a résumé crowded with achievement. Navratilova gave a hint of what was to come by winning her first 36

matches and seven tournaments, but at the year's first major—the French Open—33rd-ranked Horvath scored a stunning fourth-round upset. It would be the only time in 11 career meetings that Navratilova would fall to the Chicago native, and the loss preempted her run at a Grand Slam before it even began. But it also got her mad, serving as the impetus to the most amazing reign of dominance the sport will ever witness.

Navratilova won her next 50 matches, adding nine tournament titles along the way, among them Wimbledon (where she beat Andrea Jaeger in the final), the US Open (her first, where she topped defending champ Chris Evert), and the Australian Open, where she bested Kathy Jordan for the crown.

By the time the year was complete, Navratilova's victory chart looked more like a Rolling Stones tour schedule—in addition to the majors, there was Los Angeles, Orlando, Dallas, Chicago, Houston, Washington, D.C., Hilton

Head, Tokyo, Filderstadt, Tampa, Toronto, Eastbourne, and New York City. Okay, so maybe the Stones have never played Filderstadt.

Navratilova then hit 1984 without missing a stroke, running her streak to six straight majors by whipping Chris Evert in consecutive finals at the French Open, Wimbledon, and US Open. The Grand Slam was at her fingertips as she streaked into the Australian Open semifinals with a 74-match win streak, with Helena Sukova the fodder on the other side of the net. Navratilova captured the first set before Sukova gamely rallied for a 1-6, 6-3, 7-5 triumph to crush those dreams. (Navratilova did get a consolation prize of sorts, as she and partner Pam Shriver won the doubles Grand Slam that year.)

Undeterred, Navratilova immediately embarked on a 54-match win streak and would later run off 56 straight victories. In fact, in a span from 1981 to 1987, Navratilova lost only 14 times. It was dominance even the Harlem Globetrotters would envy...and unlike the Washington Generals, Navratilova's opponents were trying to win.

Born October 18, 1956, in Prague, Navratilova made her Tour debut in 1973 at Ft. Lauderdale, beating Gail Chanfreau in a first-round match. Later that year, the 17-year-old reached the quarterfinals at the French Open and began her intense—though friendly—rivalry with Evert in a tournament in Akron.

"Even though I'd never heard of her, and couldn't pronounce or spell her name, I could tell she'd be trouble," remarked Evert, who won that meeting but was trumped in the all-time series, 43-37.

At the 1976 US Open—shortly after being denounced by the communist Czech government for her continued "Americanization"—Navratilova announced she was defecting. She became a U.S. citizen in 1981.

Navratilova won Wimbledon in 1978, the first of nine singles titles she would earn at the All England Club and the first of 59 majors (18 singles, 31 doubles, 10 mixed) that would come her way over the ensuing 29 years. She finished with 167 career singles titles, more than any male or female player, as well as 174 doubles crowns, the last one coming in 2004 (with partner Lisa Raymond) in Vienna at the age of 48.

Success was attained not just as a result of talent, but her immense desire. As Navratilova herself once asked rhetorically, "Do you know the difference between involvement and commitment? Think of ham and eggs. The chicken is involved. The pig is committed."

And so was Martina Navratilova, who committed herself to being the greatest women's tennis player ever and who produced a year that will never be matched.

**THE LETHAL LEAD-OFF
MAN BLEW PAST LOU BROCK
AND INTO THE RECORD BOOK.**

Rickey Henderson

In the early 1980s, the late, great, ornery Billy Martin was the manager of the Oakland A's. Martin's philosophy of getting players on base and moving them from station to station by any means possible—including stolen bases—was called "Billy Ball." With a kindred spirit named Rickey Henderson as his left fielder and leadoff hitter, Martin, much like director Martin Scorsese working in the '70s with a young Robert DeNiro, had found the perfect artist to execute his vision.

Henderson ran wild in Billy Ball, and baseball history was made, 90 feet at a time.

In Henderson's first full season in the big leagues, 1980, all he did was break Ty Cobb's American League stolen-base record of 96 with a nice, even 100. Then, somehow, this team without much pop won 17 of its first 18 and skittered its way into the playoffs in 1981. Since that season was abbreviated by a players' strike, Rickey's vowed assault on Lou Brock's major league record of 118 stolen bases had to wait until 1982.

Lean but muscular at 5'10", 185 pounds, Henderson had thighs like jet turbines. He played low to the ground: batting in a crouch that reduced his strike zone to roughly 10 inches high; running the bases from a knock-kneed position designed to give him mobility and maximum propulsion; and even slamming into his ill-gotten base with an emphatic headfirst slide. "I don't hit the ground too hard," Henderson said. "I come in like an airplane."

An appreciative Martin said, "He's the most exciting player since Mickey Mantle."

Opponents didn't disagree, although they clearly didn't savor Rickey's base-path effrontery nearly as much as his manager did.

Despite his world-class short-burst speed and solid instincts, Henderson still got caught almost 25 percent of the time. Certainly, giving outs to the other team is not a desirable result, but at a certain point, the almost kamikaze nature of Henderson's forays had to become slightly unnerving for his foes.

"What separates the great base stealer from the rest is arrogance," the old master Brock explained. "You have to eliminate all fear and declare war on the entire league."

Mission accomplished. Yankee pitcher Dave Righetti called Rickey "the number one disruptive force in the American League."

He ran in close games. He ran in blowouts. He stole home, twice. He didn't care about so-called baseball "etiquette." With 84 stolen bases rung up by the All-Star break, Brock's record was in grave danger. The A's were stumbling in 1982, with critics saying that Billy Ball couldn't work in the long run, but Rickey was relentless.

The same drive that enabled him to play 25 seasons in the big leagues and set major league records for total runs scored (2,295), total stolen bases (1,406), and leadoff home runs (81) was fueling him in the quest for his first major league record.

On August 27, 1982, in Milwaukee, with the regal Brock in the stands to serve as witness,

Rickey Henderson drew a two-out, bases-empty walk in the third inning from Doc Medich. The veteran pitcher probably didn't feel like being a footnote in the history books (sorry, Doc), so he made four consecutive pickoff moves to first base, trying to keep the Man of Steal honest.

It's such a lonely word.

Medich's next throw was a pitchout to catcher Ted Simmons. Rickey ran. The catcher fired to second, straight and true. However, the breathtaking Rickey Henderson had already purloined his historic 119th stolen base.

Being the audacious showman he always was, he ripped the base out of the ground and held it aloft as 41,600 fans cheered and Brock and AL president Lee MacPhail took the field for a short ceremony. Then he stole three more bases in that game and wound up the season with a grand (larcenous) total of 130, which has never been seriously threatened since.

PERMANENT GREEN LIGHT
Oakland's Rickey Henderson was a base-path kleptomaniac in 1982, obliterating Lou Brock's single-season stolen base mark of 118 with 130.

191

BANNED FROM BOXING, THE CUBS' FIREPLUG KO'ED BASEBALL'S **RBI** RECORD.

Hack Wilson

Lewis Wilson hoped to start the year 1930 with a bang.

The Chicago Cubs outfielder, better known as "Hack," planned on staging an exhibition boxing match versus combative Chicago White Sox first baseman Art Shires. But when Commissioner Kenesaw Mountain Landis, as much a softie as his name suggests, got wind of it, he made a statement to the effect that any player who participated in "professional boxing will be regarded by this office as having permanently retired from baseball."

Short, stocky, and admittedly no stranger to the bottom of a whiskey bottle, Hack apparently decided to take his commissioner's advice, hang up the boxing gloves, and tattoo the horsehide instead. Subsequently, the numbers he put up at the plate in 1930 were mountainous indeed, and one of them still remains a summit that's proven unconquerable—191 runs batted in.

The number has rarely been assaulted in the modern era, with the closest competition coming in the 1930s from fellow Hall of Famers Lou Gehrig (184), Hank Greenberg (183), and Jimmie Foxx (175). The closest that any modern-day player has managed to come is Manny Ramirez's 165 RBIs with the high-octane Cleveland Indians of 1999.

Wilson's accomplishments that year, including a .356 batting average and 56 home runs (which stood as the National League record for 68 years, until the exploits of Mark McGwire and Sammy Sosa), were only able to lift the Cubs within two games of the pennant-winning St. Louis Cardinals.

As tall as Wilson's numbers were, he was one of the shortest men in major league history. In his fine biography, *Fouled Away: The Baseball Tragedy of Hack Wilson*, author Clifton Blue Parker wrote that Hack "was a sight to behold, perhaps the oddest-looking ballplayer ever to put a uniform on. He stood 5'6". Yet he weighed 200 pounds, with a barrel chest, blacksmith arms, and bulging thighs and calves on short legs that tapered to tiny feet—so tiny that he wore a size five-and-one-half shoe. Mounted on his massive shoulders was a lion-like head with a huge neck that required an 18-inch collar.

"He looked as if God had gotten some of the parts mixed up. Too much of this, too little of that."

But for one blessed season—when the ball was reputed to be "livelier" in order to capitalize on the mania that Babe Ruth's feats had created—this anvil-esque slugger had the swing of Zeus. He hit for the cycle. He had two three-homer games. He tied one of the Babe's records with eight multi-homer games. And in August alone, with the Cubs battling for the pennant, he pounded out 13 round-trippers and knocked in 53 runs. Strangely enough, he did not record a single grand slam on the season.

Crazier still, *The Sporting News* gave their National League Most Valuable Player award to Bill Terry of the Giants instead of Wilson. Sure, Terry turned out to be the last National Leaguer to hit .400 (.401, to be exact), but his 129 RBIs fell 62 short of Hack's eternal total! The hard-hittin' Cubbies even had another guy who bettered Terry's RBI output—outfielder Kiki Cuyler (134).

At least the Baseball Writers Association had the good sense to bequeath their "unofficial" award to Hack, and the Cubs responded in kind, giving him a $1,000 bonus and a 1931 contract for a then-lordly $35,000.

Sadly, though, that was the beginning of the end for Wilson. Although he had been immensely productive since 1926 and was just 31 years old, in 1931 he tailed off miserably. He rallied to have a few more good years, but Wilson only wound up lasting 12 years in the big leagues. He didn't live to see the Veterans Committee enshrine him in the Hall of Fame, succumbing to his alcoholism and dying penniless at 48.

Still, he did make a significant impact on the game and those who knew it. "For years," said Chicago White Sox owner Bill Veeck, "it was impossible for me to look at any round outfielder who could hit a long ball without deciding I had found myself another Hack Wilson."

THE SPLENDID SPLINTER PUT AN EXCLAMATION POINT ON BASEBALL'S LAST .400 SEASON.

Ted Williams

When is .3999955 not good enough? When you're Ted Williams.

The blossoming 23-year-old lefty slugger—in the third year of what would become a Hall of Fame career with Boston Red Sox—entered the final day of the 1941 season with what baseball officials considered a .400 batting average. So if Williams simply sat out the team's September 28 doubleheader at Philadelphia, he was assured of being the major league's first .400 hitter since Bill Terry batted .401 for the 1930 New York Giants.

Williams, though, had already grown weary of Boston's media critics, who for two years questioned everything from his personal life to his dedication to baseball. He wasn't going to give "The Knights of the Keyboard," as he later dubbed them, any more fodder. So on a dreary afternoon in front of 10,000 fans at Shibe Park, Williams went against conventional wisdom (and manager Joe Cronin's advice) and played. Both games.

And while Williams wasn't expecting any special treatment from his hosts, he probably didn't need it, either, since Connie Mack's Athletics were closing out another in a string of dismal campaigns, this one clocking in at 64-90. He tells this story in his 1969 autobiography *My Turn At Bat*: "When I came to bat for the first time that day, the Philadelphia catcher, Frankie Hayes, said, 'Ted, Mr. Mack told us if we let up on you he'll run us out of baseball. I wish you all the luck in the world, but we're not giving you a damn thing.'"

What they gave him were a lot of pitches to put into play, which is all Williams needed. He banged out four hits in the opener, including his league-leading 37th home run, pumping his average to .404 while the Sox captured a 12-11 slugfest. He was in the lineup for the nightcap as well, adding a double and single in three trips to the plate to finish the season with a .406 average. No major leaguer has hit .400 since.

It was a classic final entry in an amazing year. After batting .389 in April, Williams hit at a .436 clip in May and the chase was on. At the All-Star Game in Detroit, he belted a three-run homer that provided the American League with a 7-5 triumph. A week later, when Joe DiMaggio's record-breaking 56-game hitting streak was snapped, it was noted that DiMaggio batted .408 over that span; Williams, meanwhile, hit .412. Still, the Red Sox left fielder was not named MVP, the honor instead going to DiMaggio.

Williams's sharp eye at the plate—he claimed to be able to see the stitches on a pitched ball—remained part of his repertoire throughout his career. He batted .388 at age 39, then hit .328 the next year to become the American League's oldest batting champion. Upon retiring in 1960, he had belted 521 home runs despite missing nearly five years in the prime of his career to serve in the U.S. Armed Forces during World War II and the Korean Conflict. Williams's lifetime batting average of .344 ranks seventh all time, yet is first among anyone whose career encompassed solely the live-ball era. Most amazingly, he struck out only 709 times in more than 7,700 at-bats, proving that the thing Ted Williams struck most was often was fear in the minds of opposing pitchers.

EVERYBODY'S ALL- STAR When Ted Williams batted .406 for the Red Sox in 1941, he also slugged the game-winning home run in that year's All-Star Game.

2,003

O.J. SIMPSON

His name conjures up the oddest cross-section of images imaginable. In the 1990s, it's an accused murderer. During the 1980s, it's the luggage-hurtling pitchman for Hertz Rent-A-Car and comedic actor in *The Naked Gun* series. But whenever O.J. Simpson's name was raised during the 1970s, it was for one reason only: to place him among the NFL's greatest all-time running backs who set a standard that in some eyes can never be equaled.

The number one overall draft pick in 1969—selected by the Buffalo Bills after a Heisman-winning career at the University of Southern California—Simpson took four years to blossom. His first two pro coaches, John Rauch and Harvey Johnson, underused him, providing Simpson barely 15 touches per game as they presided over an 8-33-1 debacle between 1969 and 1971. That all changed when Lou Saban—who had taken the Bills to a pair of AFL Championships a decade earlier—returned to coach the team. He did something that had escaped the minds of his predecessors. He gave the ball to Simpson. Often.

In 1972, O.J.'s carries increased by more than 100 and he led the league in rushing for the first of four times, picking up 1,251 yards. It was merely an advance clip for the feature film that Simpson and his mates produced in 1973. Running behind an offensive line billed as "the Electric Company"—with guards Reggie McKenzie and Joe DeLamielleure, tackles Dave Foley and Donnie Green, and center Mike Montler—and playing in the newly opened Rich (now Ralph Wilson) Stadium, the Juice gave NFL defenses a beating like they never had seen. It started in the Bills' opener, a 31-13 victory at New England, in which he gained 250 yards. He topped 100 yards six times in Buffalo's first seven games, placing Jim Brown's NFL record of 1,863 yards within his reach. Simpson's linemates, however, had even loftier aspirations.

Before the season, the back had announced, "I'm going after 1,700 yards this year." McKenzie, then a confident second-year player out of Michigan, barked back, "Make it two thousand."

Simpson surpassed the first goal in Week 13 by lighting up the Patriots' defense once again, this time to the tune of 219 yards in a 37-13 home triumph. That made history possible in the team's finale, though it would need to happen on the snowy and slippery turf at Shea Stadium. He did make history that day...not once, but twice. Before the first half was complete in what would be a 34-14 win over the New York Jets, Simpson had eclipsed Brown's decade-old league standard. Then in the fourth quarter, running in the shadows of a McKenzie block, he posted a six-yard gain and became the first player to surpass 2,000 rushing yards in a season.

He finished with 2,003, averaging 6.0 yards per carry and scoring 12 times. He was named league MVP while helping the Bills to a 9-5 record, their best since joining the NFL.

A JUICY TALE Back in the day, O.J. Simpson was a household name for becoming the NFL's first single-season 2,000-yard rusher, eclipsing that milestone in the Bills' 1973 finale against the Jets.

Success in sports can often be measured by streaks. Think about it...it is one thing to be a champion, to be good at something. It is even more special when you have longevity, a length of time where you are successful.

The ability to dominate for a long period of time distinguishes good ones from great ones. Those streaks put people and teams in record books, and they simply won't be erased barring a miracle.

Some of these streaks have withstood the test of time. I know that there is great pressure when someone makes any run at a great streak. For example, think about what Pete Rose went through when he challenged Joe DiMaggio's 56-game hit streak. Night in and night out, the media would hound him, asking question after question about chasing that mark. Eventually, Rose fell short. Now when someone extends a hit streak to 30 or more games, like Chase Utley or Jimmy Rollins of the Phillies in recent years, there is the inevitable comparison to Joe Di.

I remember hearing debates when I was a kid. Members of my family would talk about Joe Di and Ted Williams. Wow, those were interesting discussions.

Think about the pressure on Cal Ripken Jr. to play every day. He went out there despite any nagging ailments, illnesses, or night games followed by day games. Yes, he passed Lou Gehrig's amazing consecutive games played streak, and I don't think in this day and age with travel, injuries, and the pressure, that anyone will come close to Ripken's mark of 2,632. He was a true iron man, always a class act on and off the field.

I can remember the number 88, with the Wizard of Westwood, John Wooden, and his UCLA Bruins dominating college basketball. Nobody will ever come close to that again, and no team has gone through an unbeaten season since Indiana did it all the way back in 1976. UCLA's magical streak was snapped on a Saturday afternoon in South Bend, Indiana. My buddy Digger Phelps and his Irish scored shock city, sending Wooden and his Bruins home with that 88-game win streak over.

I have heard about this number so many times because of Digger. It was such a dramatic finish, and Bill Walton says that loss caused one of his biggest nightmares—having to listen to Digger brag about breaking that streak!

When you think about it, 88 straight wins was so special. Wooden is as special as it gets, with the great knack of getting teams to play as a unit. It was all about TEAM with the UCLA coach—T for togetherness, E for effort, A for attitude, and M for mental toughness. That was the Bruins' story until the miracle in South Bend, when the Golden Dome shone brightly at the end of that contest. I hear about it from Mr. Phelps 10 times a year, baby!

It is not easy to go undefeated in college football these days. So imagine what an accomplishment it was for the Oklahoma Sooners in the '50s. Bud Wilkinson's team won 47 games in a row. Every opponent knew how good Oklahoma was, so you know the Sooners received everyone's best shot.

It takes the heart of a champion to win. It takes even more to do it again and again, with the pressure mounting to repeat the feat. These are truly incredible streaks, my friends.

Dick Vitale

BREAK IT UP

Outstanding Streaks

Q: WHAT DO YOU GET WHEN YOU REMOVE ONE OF THE "50 GREATEST PLAYERS IN NBA HISTORY" FROM YOUR ROSTER JUST A COUPLE WEEKS INTO THE REGULAR SEASON?

33

A: THE LONGEST WINNING STREAK IN LEAGUE HISTORY.

The Lakers

True story.

At the start of the 1971-72 season, the Los Angeles Lakers lost the legendary Elgin Baylor to retirement. At 37, Baylor felt he just couldn't compete up to his normal standards and didn't want to hold the team back. That left the team with just two more of the "50 Greatest" from the NBA's 1996 list (an aging Wilt Chamberlain and Jerry West) plus another All-Star, sharp-shooting guard Gail Goodrich, and a slew of solid role players.

Judging by the end result, it seems like it was enough.

Under new coach Bill Sharman, who had starred locally at USC and then for years with the Boston Celtics (okay, fine—he, too, was one of the "50 Greatest"), the crusty conglomeration kablomerated the rest of the league that year, roaring to the NBA title and setting a new record for most victories in a single season, with 69, against just 13 losses.

Although the 1995-96 Chicago Bulls surpassed the 69-win level, there is one record this Laker team put up that still seems untouchable. After dropping to 6-3 in early November, they proceeded to rip off a 33-game win streak, the modern-era record for any of the major professional sports in America. The previous NBA record was 20, set just the year before by the NBA champion Milwaukee Bucks, with Kareem Abdul-Jabbar and Oscar Robertson.

"The funny thing is, a lot of those games weren't even close," said Sharman. "It was just an amazing stretch."

With second-year man Jim McMillian stepping into Baylor's starting spot and Happy Hairston at the other forward, this was a well-rounded group of players who knew their roles and executed them with extreme prejudice.

At 35, Chamberlain was no longer the point-a-minute terror he had been with Philadelphia in the '60s, but he was wiser and lethally effective.

THE LAKE SHOW GETS EXTENDED Veteran guard Jerry "Mr. Clutch" West was one of the driving forces behind Los Angeles' 33-game winning streak in 1971–72.

Concentrating primarily on defense, he led the league in rebounding, wiping the glass clean at a ridiculous rate of 19.2 per game.

While the Dipper's scoring average dipped to a career low 14.8 points per game, he shot a league-leading .649 from the floor. (The following year, in his swan song, the uncanny and unmerciful Chamberlain shot .727 from the field, another league record that may never be broken.)

In retrospect, it seems likely that the 7'1" superstar encouraged the misperception that his skills were fading, as a means of self-motivation. Early on in the streak he said, "By 1980 I'll be a forgotten religion. I'll just be remembered vaguely as the guy who was lousy at the free throw line."

Likewise, West, beginning to slow down some at 33, willingly ceded some of his shots to the sweet-stroking Goodrich (who averaged 25.9 points per game) and showed that he could get a little cranky himself.

After the team barely took a squeaker against lowly Houston, West chastised himself for poor shooting. "There were midgets guarding me and I still couldn't score," he lamented.

Not that "Mr. Clutch" had lost it yet—he still averaged 25.8 points per game in 1971-72, but had been pouring in 31 a game just two years prior. With the floor spread and the diverse weapons in place, West wound up leading the league in assists, with a career-best 9.7 per game.

Some highlights from the streak:

- In win #13, a 132-113 blowout of Detroit, Wilt dominates Pistons great Bob Lanier with a double-31 (points/rebounds). "He played like he was in his second childhood," said Lanier.
- In Win #14, McMillian has the flu, and a first-time starter named Pat Riley scores 20 points as the Lakers roll, 138-121 over Seattle, and complete the first perfect month in NBA history. They're about to move on to their second.
- On December 27, 14,500 people show up at the Forum on a rainy day to watch the streaking Lakers. To watch the Lakers *practice*.

"The Lakers seem to have jelled," said Kareem, in a bit of an understatement. Although the Bucks fell once during the streak (Win #11 in Los Angeles), the defending champs were not going away.

After the Lakers had disarmed a tough Bullets team in Baltimore to eclipse baseball's 1916 New York Giants' previous all-sport record streak of 26 wins in a row, Wilt revealed that there was more pressure than just the streak. "Look at it this way," he said. "We've won 27 in a row and we're one game ahead of the damn Milwaukee Bucks." Truth be told, the lurking Bucks were actually two-and-a-half games behind in the West, but two weeks later, on January 9, 1972, they rose up and ended the historic streak in Wisconsin, 120-104, behind Abdul-Jabbar's 39 points.

"It's not the streak [ending]," said a disappointed Goodrich after the game. "It's the fact we lost to the team that's our biggest threat to a world title."

Three months later, it wasn't a problem. The Lakers got their revenge on the Bucks in the Western Conference Finals and eliminated the New York Knicks to add the NBA title to their amazing streak.

47

Oklahoma Football

OKLAHOMA FOOTBALL WAS PLAIN AWESOME IN THE 1950s.

When your state university's football program is 12 years older than the state itself, that's an impressive feat. But not nearly as impressive as a 47-game winning streak, the longest in major college history. Both form part of the University of Oklahoma's football legacy.

The school played its inaugural gridiron game in 1895, more than decade before Oklahoma was admitted as the Union's 46th state. The sport quickly became the centerpiece of the athletics program but attained its greatest success shortly after World War II. Events were put in motion in 1946 with the hiring of Jim Tatum as head coach, who brought with him an eager 29-year-old assistant named Bud Wilkinson. A decade earlier, Wilkinson had quarterbacked the University of Minnesota to three national championships.

When Tatum departed after just one season to take a similar post at Maryland, Oklahoma's Board of Regents appointed the young Wilkinson head coach. Their decision was richly rewarded. Wilkinson oversaw a 7-2-1 campaign in 1947, then led the Sooners on a 31-game winning streak between 1948 and 1950, capped by the school's first national championship.

An even more impressive streak took root in 1953. Though the year began inauspiciously with a 28-21 loss to Notre Dame and a 7-7 tie against the University of Pittsburgh, from that point Oklahoma steamrolled through opponents in a way never before seen. The run started with a 19-14 road victory against Texas; triumphs over Kansas, Colorado, Kansas State, Missouri, Iowa State, Nebraska, Oklahoma State, and Maryland all followed, that last one coming in the Orange Bowl.

It was more of the same in 1954, 1955, 1956, and again for the first seven weeks of 1957. Win #30 also was over Maryland, this one a 20-6 decision in the Orange Bowl that closed out the '55 season and sent a second national championship to Norman, Oklahoma. The Sooners captured a third national title in 1956.

Among the stars fueling those glory days were guard J.D. Roberts, the 1953 Outland Trophy winner as the nation's top interior lineman; center Kurt Burris, who finished second in the 1954 Heisman Award voting; and running back Tommy McDonald, the 1956 Maxwell Club recipient as the nation's top collegiate player.

During the streak, Oklahoma shut out 23 opponents, scored 40 or more points 21 times, and allowed more than 20 points just once (and that came in a 56-21 drubbing of the University of Colorado). Colorado, however, did become a thorn in OU's side. The Buffaloes led their 1956 meeting 19-6 at halftime before falling, 27-19, and in 1957 they took Oklahoma down to the wire in a 14-13 setback.

On November 9, 1957, a 39-14 triumph at Missouri extended the Sooners' streak to 47 games. Next up was a home date against unranked Notre Dame. Oklahoma had humiliated the Irish, 40-0, the previous year in South Bend, and there was little reason to think this meeting at Owen Field would produce anything different. Yet for better than three quarters, neither school dented the scoreboard. Finally, with less than four minutes remaining, Notre Dame's Dick Lynch powered over the goal line on a three-yard run for what turned out to be the game's only points. The Sooners' streak had come to a shocking end.

In the locker room, Wilkinson praised his team, telling them, "Men, the only people who never lose are the ones who never play the game." Any letdown was short-lived. Oklahoma bounced back to win its final three regular-season games and finished the year 10-1, thrashing Duke, 48-21, in the Orange Bowl. And the Sooners continued to dominate the Big Six Conference, running their streak to 14 straight championships before being unseated in 1960.

No Division I school has approached Oklahoma's streak in the last half century.

(photo courtesy Getty Images)

**THE YANKEE CLIPPER JOLTED THE NATION IN 1941
WITH HIS TWO-MONTH HITTING STREAK.**

Joe DiMaggio

Untouchable?

Now wait a second. For all the proclamations about Joe DiMaggio's 56-game hitting streak being one of baseball's sacred—and unattainable—records, let's remember it wasn't even the longest streak of his career.

As an 18-year-old playing for the San Francisco Seals of the Pacific Coast League, DiMaggio got base hits in 61 straight games, shattering the minor league record held by Jack Ness (49, in 1914).

"I never really felt any pressure," insisted DiMaggio. "I was just a kid. I didn't know what pressure was, and I was having too much fun."

Such a feat should lead to direct entry into the major leagues, but DiMaggio had to overcome skepticism after a career-threatening knee injury in 1934 that dissuaded the Chicago Cubs from even giving him a tryout. The Yankees thought he was still worth the gamble and dealt for him—sending $25,000 and several players to the Seals—though they kept him in San Francisco

for one more season. Fully recovered, DiMaggio tore up the PCL, winning Most Valuable Player accolades after batting .398 with 34 home runs.

On May 3, 1936, following the first in a career full of contract squabbles, DiMaggio debuted with the Yankees, taking over for what a year earlier had been a Jesse Hill–Earle Combs platoon in left field. When Ben Chapman was dealt to the Washington Senators midway through the year, DiMaggio moved to center. He had an immediate impact, batting .323 with 29 home runs and led the American League with 22 assists as New York won the World Series for the first time since 1932.

In his second season he led the majors in home runs (46); then, in 1939, he flirted with batting .400 before settling for a league-best .381. He led the AL again the following year with a .352 average.

That brings us to 1941. Not all was right in the Bronx coming into the season. The previous season had marked the first time in DiMaggio's career that New York didn't win the World Series (that distinction going to the Cincinnati Reds). Worse yet, they didn't even capture the American League pennant. The malaise seemed to carry over. On May 15, their record stood at an un-Yankee-like 14-14 and DiMaggio was stuck in a batting funk. Even when he got one hit in four at-bats that afternoon against White Sox lefty Eddie Smith, it was hardly anything of note since it came during a 13-1 shellacking.

But with two hits the next day, one more the day after that, and then a 3-for-3 game at St. Louis, DiMaggio found a groove. He built up his streak against the likes of Schoolboy Rowe and future Hall of Famers Lefty Grove, Bob Feller, and Hal Newhouser. On June 2—the day of former teammate Lou Gehrig's death—it reached 19 games.

"That's when I became conscious of the streak," said DiMaggio. "But [even] at that stage, I didn't think too much of it."

On June 16, with a double off the Indians' Al Milnar, he tied the Yankees' record of 29 straight games. His next focus became George Sisler's American League mark of 41, which he broke on June 29 with a double off the Senators' Red Anderson. On July 2 at Yankee Stadium, DiMaggio shattered the major league mark of 44, held by Willie Keeler since 1897, by drilling a three-run homer against Boston's Dick Newsome.

DiMaggio didn't take time off to soak up any adulation, and he certainly didn't suffer a letdown. In fact, he did his best hitting after passing Keeler, going 24-of-45 over the next 11 games. On July 16 at Cleveland's League Park, he banged out three more hits to extend his streak to 56.

The end came, finally, on July 17, 1941. Playing again in Cleveland, this time under the lights at Municipal Stadium, a crowd of 67,468 twice saw Indians third baseman Ken Keltner rob DiMaggio of hits. In his final at-bat, Lou Boudreau handled a shot up the middle that was turned into an inning-ending double play. The streak was over, but DiMaggio immediately followed it with another one that lasted 17 games, giving him base hits in an astounding 73 out of 74 games.

JOLT OF ELECTRICITY Joe DiMaggio drives a single to left in the latter stages of his 56-game hitting streak that captivated the nation in 1941.

59.0

THE **BULLDOG** BREAKS ANOTHER **DODGER'S**
DECADES OLD RECORD

Orel Hershiser

There was a reason Tommy Lasorda nick-named Orel Hershiser "Bulldog."

It wasn't because of the Los Angeles Dodgers pitcher's glasses, his neat haircut, and his All-American, Richie Cunningham demeanor. It wasn't because of the physique, which his own father described as featuring "that sunken chest of his."

Actually, it kind of was about those three things. Plus, it was about his young pitcher's rather un-jock-ified name. But in the end, it was because of his persistence. His stubbornness. His refusal to give in.

For the stretch run of one glorious pennant race in 1988, the Bulldog bowed to no one, with a string of sparkling performances that shackled opponents' bats, landed him in the record books, and helped catapult his team to World Series glory. Narrowly topping the record set by another Dodgers great, Don Drysdale, Hershiser held opposing teams scoreless for 59 consecutive innings. The streak ran through the entire month of September, with five complete-game shutouts to his credit en route to a Cy Young Award season.

88

BREWING UP A STAGGERING WINNING STREAK IN THE 1970s.

UCLA Basketball

Nowadays, the college basketball program most associated with ongoing success is Duke. But a few generations ago, the four letters that signified dominance were U-C-L-A.

It's tough to wrap one's mind around how good the Bruins were in a 12-year stretch from 1963-64 through 1974-75. But we'll give it a try: a 335-22 (.938) record; 10 NCAA championships; four undefeated seasons; and, get this, an 88-game—yes, as in double snowmen—win streak.

The architect of it all was John Wooden, who had taken charge of the UCLA program in 1948 after a two-year stint at Indiana State. At the time, the Bruins were hardly a power on the hardwood. "The Wizard of Westwood" changed all that. He went 22-7 his first year, won 24 games in his second season, and from then on consistently fielded teams among the nation's best.

UCLA made the jump to dynasty in the 1963-64 season when guard Walt Hazzard starred for a 30-0 squad that captured the program's first NCAA title by defeating—curiously enough—Duke. Gail Goodrich fueled a second straight championship in the 1965-66 season. Though they missed the NCAAs the following season, that momentary pause was followed by a staggering seven consecutive national titles.

Lew Alcindor—known by today's fans as NBA all-time scoring leader Kareem Abdul-Jabbar—played center for UCLA's three championship teams from 1967 to 1969. The school's title count kept increasing with the likes of Steve Patterson, Curtis Rowe, and Sidney Wicks.

Midway through the 1970-71 campaign, Wooden's Bruins were beaten by Notre Dame, 89-82, in what proved to be their lone setback en route to a fifth straight NCAA championship. Nearly three calendar years passed before they lost again. Bill Walton, the irreverent, redheaded center from La Mesa, California, was a big reason why. He was a sophomore in 1971-72 when UCLA finished 30-0 and won its games by an average of 30 points; the Bruins duplicated that mark in 1972-73, during which they passed the Division I record of 60 straight wins that had been held by the University of San Francisco. When they beat Memphis State in the NCAA championship game, Walton shot 21-of-22 from the field and scored 44 points.

UCLA burst out to a 14-0 start in Walton's senior season to grow the streak to 88 games. On January 19, 1974, they traveled to South Bend and appeared to fend off a feisty Notre Dame team that was ranked number two in the country. Walton, playing despite a bad back that

had sidelined him the previous two weeks, netted 24 points in helping the Bruins build a 70-59 lead with 3:32 remaining. They wouldn't score again.

After Notre Dame's John Shumate hit a shot over Walton and then got a layup off a steal, it was 70-63. Another steal sent Adrian Dantley in on a fast break to make it 70-65 with 2:22 to play. Irish guard Gary Brokaw followed by knocking down back-to-back jumpers to slice the deficit to one. Keith Wilkes appeared to answer for UCLA, but his basket was waved off after an offensive foul. Notre Dame got the ball back and

UPSET BRUIN Coach John Wooden huddles with his team during the final timeout of the 1974 loss to Notre Dame that snapped UCLA's 88-game winning streak.

looked for the 6'8" Shumate, who was blanketed inside. Instead, the pass went to Dwight "the Ice Man" Clay, whose corner jumper with 29 seconds remaining put the Irish ahead.

With the Athletic and Convocation Center crowd now in a delirious state, Wooden called a timeout and drew up a play for Walton. Instead, Tommy Curtis took the shot and missed. Dave Meyers's follow-up didn't fall, either, but the Bruins kept possession when the ball bounced out of play off a defender's leg. Off the inbounds pass, Walton took a shot and missed—his only misfire in seven second-half attempts. Tips by Pete Trgovich and Meyers came up empty. Maybe a leprechaun was guarding the basket. Finally Shumate grabbed hold of the loose ball as time expired. Final score: Notre Dame 71, UCLA 70.

"What bothered me about the loss...was how we lost and the fact we went dead in the final three minutes," said Wooden. "Notre Dame scored 12 straight points and I didn't think that was possible against any team with Bill Walton on it."

The Bruins exacted revenge and regained their number-one ranking the following week by pounding the Irish, 94-75, at Pauley Pavilion. But with that air of invincibility gone, they wouldn't win an eighth straight NCAA championship. North Carolina State knocked them out in the semifinals.

Wooden stayed one more year and performed one of his finest coaching jobs in 1974-75 as UCLA finished 28-3 and reclaimed the NCAA title by beating Kentucky, 92-85, in the final.

Occasionally forgotten with all his coaching success is that Wooden was first a terrific player.

STAR CENTER BILL WALTON pulls down a rebound at the height of the streak in January 1972. (photo courtesy Getty Images)

Three times he earned All-America honors at Purdue, and in 1932 he was chosen as the College Basketball Player of the Year. He gained induction into the National Basketball Hall of Fame in 1961—as a player.

Still, it's coaching that won Wooden his greatest fame, and in 2000 he was named the Naismith Men's College Coach of the Century. It doesn't get much better than that—just like it didn't get any better than U-C-L-A.

107

WITH POWER AND POISE HE **DOMINATED** A DECADE

Edwin Moses

The great biblical figure Moses was renowned for his persistence (see, "Desert, Wandering in for 40 years") and his ability to overcome major hurdles (see, "Sea, Red"). The great track and field figure Moses (Edwin) was pretty strong in those categories himself.

On August 26, 1977, Germany's Harald Schmid defeated the 22-year-old Moses in the 400-meter intermediate hurdles, but after that day, the elegant and enigmatic Moses reigned supreme over this event for almost a decade. The two-time Olympic champion generated one of the most leviathan winning streaks in modern sporting history, going undefeated in 122 straight races and 107 straight finals over the course of nine years, nine months, and nine days.

Born in Dayton, Ohio, in 1955, this son of educator parents received an academic scholarship as a physics and engineering major at Morehouse College. Athletically, dalliances with team sports in high school hadn't been satisfactory, but then Moses found his home on the oval.

"I found that I enjoyed individual sports much more," he said. "Everything is cut and dry; nothing is arbitrary. It's just a matter of getting to the finish line first."

At Morehouse, the 6'2", 185-pound Moses became known as the Bionic Man, due to both his intense workouts and his use of scientific method to keep track of the results and plot better techniques. With his long, loping stride spanning nearly 10 feet, he also dared to revolutionize the sport, knocking the traditional 14-step interval between hurdles to 13.

It worked. As of late March 1976, Moses had run the 400-meter hurdles just once, his specialties to that being point the 110-meter hurdles and the 400-meter sprint. But a few months later, at the 1976 Montreal Olympics, he blazed to gold in world-record fashion with a time of 47.64 seconds (bettering John Akii-Bua's 47.82 seconds).

A star had been self-made. A week after being bested by Schmid in 1977, he avenged his loss, winning by 15 meters, and never looked back.

As the wins began to mount, disappointment came in another form—the U.S. boycott of the 1980 Moscow Olympics, which almost certainly cost Moses another gold. That year, competing mostly against himself, he broke his own world record, posting a time of 47.13 seconds in Milan.

He sat out the entire 1982 season with injuries and illness, and critics whispered that age must be catching up to the great Moses. Instead, he came back in 1983 and on his 28th birthday broke his own world record yet again, with a clocking (47.02 seconds) that stood for nine years.

In 1984 he took Olympic gold once more, in Los Angeles. At the time, he'd won 90 straight finals and held a monopolistic 17 of the 18 fastest times in his event.

He sat out the 1985 season with another injury, and when he returned he ran less frequently and not always against the top hurdlers, perhaps starting to guard his streak like aging heavyweights protect their title from young sluggers.

Finally, on June 4, 1987, in Madrid, Danny Harris ran a 47.56 to beat Moses, who atypically clipped the last hurdle with his foot.

At 31, Moses was a gentleman about the loss. "I never felt bad about losing, just about not running well," he said. "I knew it would take a superior performance to beat me, and it did. So I can't be unhappy about it. It was a good race for me."

MOSES ALONE... For more than nine years, covering 122 races and 107 finals, 400-meter hurdler Edwin Moses always broke the tape first.

2,130/2,632

Gehrig/Ripken JUST A COUPLE OF EVERYDAY SUPERSTARS.

Forget penciling in your starters. If your baseball team was lucky enough to have Lou Gehrig or Cal Ripken Jr., you could write their name in with permanent marker.

The two baseballers own the longest consecutive games-played streaks in sports history: between 1925 and 1939, Gehrig trotted out for 2,130 straight games with the Yankees, while six decades later Ripken bettered that standard by appearing in a superhuman 2,632 in a row for the Orioles.

Beyond their fraternal qualities on the field, both legends similarly earned high marks for character. The dignified and Columbia-educated Gehrig gladly remained in the background while teammates—most notably Babe Ruth—sought to make the most of the Big Apple's media spotlight. Ripken was perhaps more affable after being raised in the game (his father, Cal Sr., was a player and coach), but he staked his reputation behind a fundamentally sound, team-first approach.

Gehrig was the son of German immigrants and studied for two years at Columbia, where he starred for the Lions' football and baseball teams, before signing with Yankees in 1923. After a couple of short stints in the Bronx, he permanently made the big-league club out of spring training in 1925. His amazing streak started unamazingly enough on June 1 of that year with a pinch-hit fly out.

But the next day, he was in manager Miller Huggins's starting lineup, replacing veteran first baseman Wally Pipp, who had been plunked during batting practice and was rendered semi-conscious. Pipp was no journeyman—he carried a career .280 average and once led the team in home runs—but he had been slumping, and there was a chorus of whispers that Gehrig would soon take his spot. Instead of being jealous, he helped the young Yank gain confidence on the field (for if Gehrig had one hole in his game, it was with the glove). Batting sixth that day against the Washington Senators, Gehrig delivered three hits and was flawless in nine chances at first base.

While no one questioned Gehrig's potential, there was suspicion—likely because of his college background—that he couldn't make pro baseball's grade. "Only Lou's willingness and lack of conceit will make him into a complete ballplayer," commented Huggins. "That and those muscles are all he has."

It was more than enough. Gehrig climbed into the Yankees' clean-up hitter role and gained the nickname "Iron Horse" for his unmatched durability. When New York captured the 1927 World Series title—a season remembered by many for Ruth's 60-home run tirade—Gehrig banged out 47 round-trippers of his own and hit .373.

In 1931 he set an American League record by driving in 184 runs, a mark that still stands more than 75 years later. He smacked four home runs in a 1932 contest against the Athletics and in 1934 won the league's Triple Crown, batting

LET'S PLAY TWO THOUSAND Yankees first baseman Lou Gehrig was baseball's original iron man, before the Orioles' Cal Ripken Jr. (photo, page 73) eclipsed his mark for consecutive games played.

.363 with 49 home runs and 165 RBIs. And he wasn't immune to injury: Gehrig played through the pain of a broken thumb, a broken toe, and torturous back spasms.

Yet when his production declined in 1938—though he still hit 29 home runs and batted .295—fans, teammates, and Gehrig himself wondered what was wrong. No one was writing it off as a slump either, for the 35-year-old struggled to accomplish even routine tasks.

Gehrig worked even harder, but his condition worsened. On May 2, 1939, nine games into the season and 2,130 after becoming a fixture on the Yankees' lineup card, he confided to manager Joe McCarthy that it was time for him to sit down. Lou Gehrig would never play again. He ended his career with 493 home runs, 23 grand slams among them, and a lifetime batting average of .340.

By June, the worst-feared diagnosis came true—Gehrig had incurable amyotrophic lateral sclerosis (ALS), a hardening of the spinal cord that prevents the brain from coordinating actions with the muscles. In a ceremony that July, the Yankees retired his No. 4, while the nation's baseball writers, noting his deteriorating health, waived the normal waiting period for Hall of Fame induction. On June 2, 1941, 16 years to the day after replacing Pipp as the Yankees' first baseman, Lou Gehrig passed away.

Little did anyone suspect it possible, but baseball's longevity torch would be passed along to Cal Ripken. The Orioles' second-round draft pick—originally a pitching prospect—reached the major leagues at age 20 and commenced his streak in 1982, the same year he earned American League Rookie of the Year honors. In 1983

he was named league MVP, batting .318 with 27 home runs for the World Series champions.

While Gehrig handled the relative simple chores of first base, the 6'4" Ripken took the field each day at the physically challenging shortstop position. With his size, he was an anomaly there, especially to fans who had grown up watching Dave Concepción, Luis Aparicio, Larry Bowa, and the Orioles' own Mark Belanger. Yet Ripken's smooth fielding, which included a pair of Gold Glove Awards, paved the way for bigger ballplayers to be accepted at the position.

Ripken also experienced ailments along the way, including a severely sprained ankle and a bruised right knee, but on September 6, 1995—with an audience that included President Bill Clinton—he broke the iron-man mark in a game against the Angels. And he was up for the show, belting a home run in Baltimore's 4-2 triumph. Once the record became official after the top of the fifth inning, a banner reading "2131" was unfurled on the facade of the warehouse that stands just beyond right field at Baltimore's Camden Yards. Ripken received seven standing ovations before taking a "victory" lap around the park, high-fiving every fan he could reach.

Addressing the crowd, he said, "Tonight, I stand here overwhelmed as my name is likened with the great and courageous Lou Gehrig. I'm truly humbled to have our names spoken in the same breath."

On Sunday, September 20, 1998, in the Orioles' final home game of the season—poetically against the Yankees—Ripken was not in the lineup. It had been 2,632 games since the Orioles took the field without him. He was far from done, however, and played three more seasons, collecting his 3,000th hit in 2000. In January 2007, Ripken gained induction into the Hall of Fame.

He reflected on his accomplishment in his autobiography *The Only Way I Know*. "Breaking Lou Gehrig's record had nothing to do with extraordinary talent, which I don't have, or a bionic body, which I don't have either. Or a burning desire for the spotlight, which can be fun at times and is really gratifying, but has its drawbacks as well. I have to agree with Billy's [Ripken's] blunt conclusion. Billy knows me because he's my younger brother, and he knows baseball because he's also a major leaguer, and he says I broke that record because I could."

Both Lou Gehrig and Cal Ripken could. But, even better, they did.

Over the years numbers have played a major role in sports.

I'm talking about numbers on the backs of the jerseys. When you talk about uniform numbers, the No. 7 was always special to me. It lights me up because I think of greatness, and I think about Mickey Mantle. It has always been a special number for me, and many athletes wear that number. Over the years John Elway, Phil Esposito, Pete Maravich in the NBA...lots of stars put on that number!

My grandsons asked me what number they should wear...I said No. 7, baby! Every granddaddy feels that way! I also like that little luck factor, so I like seven and 11! I guess I am a little superstitious.

I have always said I love college basketball because the most important name is on the front of the jersey and not on the back of it. Kids play for Duke, North Carolina, Kentucky, and UCLA; the pros play for their name. Many numbers on the jersey stand out.

No. 23...Michael the Magnificent.

No. 99...The Great One, Wayne Gretzky.

I have heard many interesting stories about why players wear a certain number. Sometimes it is because of a family member. Maybe it is because of a player they idolized growing up. Sometimes it deals with superstition, just like me!

No matter the reason, some numbers simply stand out. Some are retired because of the greatness of the athletes that wore them. Kids today go out and buy sports jerseys like crazy, often because of that special uniform number. You see the number 23—but now it is LeBron James instead of that Jordan jersey.

One powerful number that stands out in my mind is 42—Jackie Robinson. It is now displayed prominently in major league baseball ballparks across America and rightfully so. Robinson's impact was so great on society, not just baseball. I can't imagine what he went through in breaking the color barrier in baseball. He was a hero to athletes and a nation. Honoring No. 42 was the right move by Major League Baseball, retiring it to signify its meaning and their appreciation for the courage of a special, special man.

So many numbers, so much meaning. Think about how many great athletes wore No. 32. Jim Brown, Sandy Koufax, Karl Malone, Steve Carlton, Bill Walton, Marcus Allen, Franco Harris. And the list goes on and on.

No. 9 is a great one: Ted Williams, Gordie Howe, Bobby Hull, Reggie Jackson, with those swinging A's!

What about lucky No. 13? Wilt Chamberlain. Dan Marino.

No. 6: Bill Russell, Stan Musial, Dr. J.—Julius Erving.

There were a lot of stars in No. 8: Cal Ripken Jr., Yogi Berra, Troy Aikman, Steve Young, Willie Stargell, Joe Morgan.

No. 33 was worn by Larry Bird, Kareem Abdul-Jabbar, Patrick Ewing, Scottie Pippen, Tony Dorsett, Eddie Murray...and many other stars.

You can sit and argue, debating night and day about the greatest to wear certain jersey numbers in various sports. No. 4—Bobby Orr, Lou Gehrig, Brett Favre.

You get the idea... Wow...

Dick Vitale

THE SHIRTS OFF THEIR BACKS

*The Numbers of the Players Who Changed
the Games They Played—Forever.*

THE INTIMIDATOR STEERED
AUTO RACING ONTO A TRACK OF
UNPRECEDENTED POPULARITY.

3

Dale Earnhardt

In a sport where one challenges mortality on a weekly basis, Dale Earnhardt rose to the ranks of immortals.

With images that remain intact years after his tragic death—his black No. 3 Chevrolet; his trademark sunglasses, mustache, and wide grin; and a brazen demeanor that rightfully earned him the moniker "the Intimidator"—Earnhardt embodied the essence of stock-car racing and galvanized its fans. He became a legendary figure they could reach out and touch, and who in turn touched them back.

Even adversaries placed Earnhardt in such high regard that in 1998, when he finally won the Daytona 500 (the premier stop on the NASCAR circuit), drivers and pit crews alike lined up to salute him during his ride to the victory lane.

"He was Elvis and John Wayne and Steve McQueen and Christa McAuliffe all melded into one bad SOB," opined ESPN.com's Marty Smith.

And the badder he was, the better he became. Seven times Earnhardt captured the season-long Winston (now NEXTEL) Cup, a title equivalent to that sport's Super Bowl champion. Only the equally legendary Richard Petty can match his total. During Earnhardt's 27-year career, he pulled into the winner's circle an extraordinary 76 times.

The Kannapolis, North Carolina, native was born with racing in his blood and followed in the footsteps of his father, Ralph, onto the stock-car circuit. He made his Winston Cup debut in 1975, taking 22nd in the World 600 at Charlotte. His big break, though, came in 1979 when at age 28 he joined Rod Osterlund's driving team. After taking his first checkered flag at Bristol and later earning his first pole at Riverside, Earnhardt was named NASCAR Rookie of the Year.

He surged to the front of the pack in 1980 by claiming his inaugural Winston Cup title after scoring five victories and 19 top-five finishes. Soon after, he shifted gears and joined Richard Childress's team, a relationship that would be rekindled and made permanent in 1984. It was then that Earnhardt's driving career truly flourished—he won six Winston Cup titles over a nine-year span, highlighted by 11 race victories in 1987 and nine more in 1990.

Despite being flooded with accolades and acclaim, for two decades Daytona had menaced him—racing's biggest jewel was still absent from Earnhardt's crown.

Of all years, 1998 seemed the most unlikely for him to break that luckless spell. Earnhardt arrived there in the throes of a 59-race winless streak, which included the Southern 500 when he inexplicably blacked out on the first lap. Even his most ardent supporters were whispering that the 46-year-old's best days were in the rearview mirror. Although a ninth straight triumph in Daytona's 125-mile qualifier encouraged a few fans, others noted that they had seen this before only to be disappointed on race day.

Yet once the pace car got out of the way, Earnhardt's famous No. 3 flew around the track on a mission. Perhaps it was the good-luck penny received from a wheelchair-bound little girl on race day who insisted it would bring victory. "We took that penny and glued it on the dashboard," he later said.

Earnhardt bolted into the lead for good on lap 140 and the chess match that ensued saw him brilliantly fight off rushes from 1997 champion Jeff Gordon, Bobby Labonte, Jeremy Mayfield, and, lastly, Rusty Wallace down the stretch.

Earnhardt's emotions afterward were simple and heartfelt. "Yes! Yes! Yes!" he exclaimed to an adoring crowd. "Twenty years! Can you believe it?

Sadly, it was on Daytona's track where Earnhardt lost his life in a tragedy for the world to see. On the final turn of the final lap of the 2001 race—which saw him battling, among others, his son Dale Jr. for victory—there was contact that caused Earnhardt to momentarily lose control. Just as he appeared to regain his bearings, he was hit again, this collision sending his car nose-first into the wall at a high rate of speed before sliding back down the track. By the time EMT's arrived, there was little they could do; Dale Earnhardt was pronounced dead hours later.

Grief spread across the entire sports community and beyond. Tributes followed—drivers and fans would in unison flash three fingers at races. Perhaps the greatest tribute, though, came from Dale Jr., who won the Daytona 500 six years to the day after his father's breakthrough triumph. Once again an Earnhardt's final lap at Daytona was a victory lap.

TRIUMPH AND TRAGEDY In 1998 Dale Earnhardt captured his first Daytona 500. Three years later, on the same Florida track, the legendary NASCAR driver lost his life in a final-lap crash.

Bobby Orr

BOSTON'S BLUE LINE LEGEND
TURNED THE GAME OF HOCKEY
ON ITS SIDE.

For mathematicians, the sideways number 8 represents the concept of infinity. For Boston hockey fans, the sideways number 4 will always represent infinite joy.

That's because the jersey belonging to Bobby Orr, the Hall of Fame defenseman who many argue was the greatest player in NHL history, went famously horizontal after ripping home the Stanley Cup-winning goal versus the St. Louis Blues in 1970.

If you think that LeBron James, Venus Williams, and Tiger Woods were mind-blowing *wunderkinds*, then try this one on for size—Orr's future services were locked up by prescient Bruins scout Wren Blair when the kid was all of 12 years old, dominating older Bantam players as a Pee-Wee in Parry Sound, Ontario.

In 1967, the crew-cut comet won the Calder Trophy (Rookie of the Year) at age 18. He would have broken in even earlier, but for the league's age restrictions. Harry Howell, the New York Ranger who won the Norris Trophy that year as the top defenseman, said he was espe-cially glad to win, "Because Orr will own this trophy from now on."

Bobby hauled home the hardware for the next eight straight seasons and redefined the role of the defenseman in modern hockey with his blaz-ing end-to-end charges and brilliant passing. He was an innovative defender, whose uncanny puck control was also used to kill major chunks of penalty time. Breaking with convention, he would skate forward toward the defensive zone, a tactic which confused opposing attackers and often caused them to avoid one-on-one rushes.

"He changed the sport by redefining the parameters of his position," wrote E.M. Swift in *Sports Illustrated*. "A defenseman, as interpreted by Orr, became both a defender and an aggressor, both a protector and a producer. Orr was more than an opportunist: he created opportunities."

In 1969-70, an already electrifying Orr broke new ice, doubling his scoring output from the previous season and posting 120 points to become the first and only defenseman ever to lead the NHL in scoring. He also won the first of his three consecutive Hart Trophies (MVP) and led the formerly moribund Bruins to the championship, capped by that game-winning shot and the famous celebratory image, forever frozen in time.

After that, the age of Orr broke through at the bank, too, with the young superstar signing hockey's first-ever $1 million contract—$200,000 per annum for five years. The Bruins got their money's worth. The next season the statistics were even more incredible, as he tallied 102 assists and 139 points with an omnipresent plus-minus rating of plus-124. After Boston knocked off the New York Rangers for their second Stanley Cup victory in 1971-72, (guess who had the game-winning goal again?), the Rangers' Rod Gilbert said, "Hockey is a team game, right? One man is not supposed to beat a whole team."

In 1974-75 the one-man crew lit the lamp 46 times—setting a record for defensemen at the time—and led the league with 135 points. The only NHL players to finish their careers with a higher points-per-game average than his 1.39 were Wayne Gretzky, Mario Lemieux, and Mike Bossy—front-liners all.

And No. 4 did all this despite a bum knee that began deteriorating in his rookie season. He went under the knife more than a dozen times during his career to try to sustain his legendary speed and mobility, but it turned out that bone-against-bone was the only competition he couldn't win. After the goal-scoring spree of 1974-75, he was never the same, and he parted ways with the Bruins in a botched negotiation that was fraught with miscommunication. A hobbled Orr retired in 1979. The Hall of Fame waived its customary three-year waiting period and ushered Orr into immortality that very year at age 31.

THE AGE OF ORR Legendary Boston defenseman Bobby Orr not only changed the Bruins' fortunes with this Stanley Cup–clinching goal in 1970—he also changed the way hockey was played.

42

IN BREAKING BASEBALL'S COLOR BARRIER, HE SHOWED MORE THAN COURAGE.

Jackie Robinson

It wasn't by chance that Jackie Robinson became the first African American to reach the modern-day major leagues. He was chosen. Make that very carefully chosen by Branch Rickey, the forward-thinking Dodgers president who fought to reintegrate America's pastime.

The year was 1945, an era when the country was still segregated, and Rickey hid his true intentions from league owners, media, and fans by stating he was exploring the possibility of placing a Negro League team at Brooklyn's Ebbets Field. What he was really doing was searching for the right player—one with the talent, maturity, and temperament to withstand the ugliness and hatred certain to be cast upon the person who broke baseball's color barrier.

Rickey heard good things about the 26-year-old Robinson, who had been a sensational four-sport athlete at UCLA, served as an army lieutenant during World War II, and starred for the Kansas City Monarchs of the Negro League. Respected *Pittsburgh Courier* sports editor Wendell Smith, who earlier that year had arranged for Robinson and fellow Negro League standouts Sam Jethroe and Marvin Williams to get a tryout with the Red Sox, further advocated on his behalf.

In August of 1945 Robinson traveled to Brooklyn to meet with Rickey, where the Dodgers executive bombarded him with questions aimed at testing his resolve. Robinson gave an account of their exchange in his 1972 autobiography *I Never Had It Made*: "'Mr. Rickey,' I asked, 'are you looking for a Negro who is afraid to fight back?' 'Robinson,' he said, 'I'm looking for a ballplayer with guts enough not to fight back.'"

By the time the meeting was over, Rickey was convinced he had the right man. He signed Robinson to a contract and assigned him to the Montreal Royals, the team's Triple-A affiliate, for the 1946 season. Robinson thrived north of the border, hitting .349 and stealing 40 bases. He then went to spring training in Havana, Cuba, where the Royals and Dodgers were working together prior to the 1947 season.

When a group of Dodgers players circulated a petition stating they would not play if Robinson made the team, Rickey immediately squashed that insubordination. He then hoped Robinson's strong play in spring training—he hit .625 with seven stolen bases in seven games against the Dodgers—would cause team members to advocate for him.

When that didn't happen, Rickey sought to put manager Leo Durocher in front of the press to say that the Dodgers could win the pennant if they had a strong first baseman, and that Robinson—who had learned the position the previous year—was the best candidate. But before Durocher was able to make such a pronouncement, Commissioner Happy Chandler suspended him for the year for "conduct detrimental to baseball" resulting from an incident the previous season.

That news, however, allowed Rickey to spring into action. Seeking to push the Durocher story out of the papers, he made history on the morning of April 9, 1947, with a simple one-sentence release: "Brooklyn announces the purchase of the contract of Jack Roosevelt Robinson from Montreal. Signed, Branch Rickey."

Baseball was about to change forever, though by box-score standards Robinson's debut on April 15, 1947, was anything but spectacular. With 25,623 on hand at Ebbets Field, No. 42 went hitless against the Boston Braves' Johnny Sain.

"If they expected any miracles out of [me], they were sadly disappointed," Robinson wrote. "I was in another slump. I grounded out to the third baseman, flied out to left field, bounced into a double play, was safe on an error, and, later, was removed as a defensive safeguard."

He was still struggling later that month when the Phillies visited for a three-game series. While Robinson had grown accustomed to insults hurled from the opposing dugout, Philadelphia manager Ben Chapman was particularly cruel in his abuse. It got so bad that it nearly pushed Robinson over the edge; he considered charging the Phillies' bench, aware that such an action would probably end his career and set back integration...both in the sport and in the country.

"Then I thought of Mr. Rickey—how his family and friends had begged him not to fight for me and my people," wrote Robinson. "I thought of all his predictions, which had come true. Mr. Rickey had come to a crossroads and made a lonely decision. I was at a crossroads. I would make mine. I would stay."

The team soon rallied around their new teammate, and Pee Wee Reese, a Kentucky native and the Dodgers' star shortstop, took the rookie under his wing. And Durocher's prediction came true. Brooklyn finished the season 94-60 and captured its first National League pennant since 1941; Robinson batted .297 and was voted Rookie of the Year.

He subsequently moved to second base and in 1949—after hitting a league-best .342 and swiping 37 bases—he was selected the National League's Most Valuable Player. He would play 10 seasons, helping the Dodgers to the 1955 World Series title and retiring with a .311 career average.

Jackie Robinson's legacy now lives on in every ballpark. In 1997, on the 50th anniversary of his reaching the major leagues, baseball permanently retired his No. 42.

Jerseys to Remember

Baseball

0—Al Oliver: The "Hit Man" zeroed in on nine straight .300 seasons between 1976 and 1984.

1/8—Eddie Gaedel: In 1951 the 3'7" squirt signed a contract with the St. Louis Browns and became the smallest person to appear in a major sports league.

1—Ozzie Smith: The "Wizard of Oz" won 13 straight Gold Gloves at shortstop between 1980 and 1992.

2—Derek Jeter: Current-day Yankees captain is a poster boy for how the game should be played and constantly places among league leaders in hits, runs, and batting average.

3—Babe Ruth: The 714 home runs are easy to remember, but did you know he was also twice a 20-game winner while pitching for the Red Sox?

4—Lou Gehrig: Played in 2,130 straight games and became first baseball player to have his number retired when the Yankees did so in 1939.

5—Johnny Bench: Perhaps the greatest catcher of all time, he won two World Series with the Reds and retired with 389 home runs.

5—Joe DiMaggio: Three-time American League MVP who had a 56-game hitting streak and is regarded as the game's greatest all-around player.

5—Brooks Robinson: Third baseman won 16 straight Gold Glove Awards (1960-75) and was MVP of the 1970 World Series.

5—Albert Pujols: Baseball's best all-tools player of the early 21st century who hit over .300 with at least 30 home runs in each of his first six major league seasons.

6—Stan Musial: Appeared in 24 All-Star Games and had 3,630 hits while belting 475 home runs.

7—Mickey Mantle: Three-time AL MVP was among the most popular ballplayers in history and holds the record with 18 World Series home runs.

7—John Neves: Spell this minor leaguer's last name backwards, and you'll see why he's on the list.

8—Yogi Berra: Quotable backstop appeared in 14 World Series, winning 10 of them, and was three-time American League MVP.

8—Cal Ripken Jr.: Shortstop/third baseman appeared in major league-record 2,632 consecutive games and was American League MVP in 1983 and 1991.

8—Carl Yastrzemski: Eighteen-time All-Star won the American League Triple Crown in 1967.

9—Minnie Minoso: Seven-time All-Star played professional baseball in seven different decades and at age 53 is the oldest player in history to get a base hit.

09—Benito Santiago: 1987 National League Rookie of the Year donned unusual version of this number in 1991 and wore it for the next three years until taking No. 18 with the Reds in 1995.

9—Ted Williams: Last major leaguer to bat .400 in a season who smashed 521 career homers despite losing five seasons while serving in the armed forces.

14—Ernie Banks: The hard-hitting Cubs shortstop/first baseman, famous for his "Let's play two" catchphrase, swatted five grand slams during the 1955 season.

14—Larry Doby: American League's first African American player, signed by the Indians in 1947, played 13 seasons and batted .283 with 253 home runs.

17—Carlos May: Ten-year major leaguer is the only major league player to wear his birthday (May 17) on the back of his jersey.

19—Bob Feller: Hard-throwing righty led American League in wins six times, fired three no-hitters, and had 12 one-hitters.

20—Mike Schmidt: Won 10 Gold Gloves, hit 548 home runs, and was three-time National League MVP.

21—Roger Clemens: Seven-time Cy Young Award winner who twice has struck out 20 batters in a game.

21—Roberto Clemente: Twelve-time Gold Glove winner had career average of .317 and was National League's 1966 MVP.

24—Willie Mays: First player in major league history to reach 500 home runs and 3,000 hits; retired with 660 career home runs and also led the NL in stolen bases four times.

29—Rod Carew: Seven-time American League batting champion hit a career-high .388 in 1977 and led the AL in batting in 1972 without hitting a home run.

32—Steve Carlton: Baseball's first four-time Cy Young Award winner holds career record for strikeouts by National Leaguer with 4,000.

32—Sandy Koufax: Three-time Cy Young Award recipient threw four no-hitters and had a career ERA of 0.95 in World Series play.

34—Nolan Ryan: Baseball's all-time strikeout king with 5,714 threw an amazing seven no-hitters and 12 more one-hitters.

42—Jackie Robinson*: See pg 80.

44—Hank Aaron: Retired from the game in 1976 as baseball's all-time leader in home runs (755) and RBIs (2,297) and was also a three-time Gold Glove Award winner.

44—Reggie Jackson: Baseball's "Mr. October" was something special the rest of the year, too, hitting 563 career home runs to help his teams reach the postseason 11 times.

THE SHIRTS OFF THEIR BACKS

45—Bob Gibson: Eight-time All-Star had a 1.12 ERA in 1968, the best in baseball's modern era.

72—Carlton Fisk: Wore the unusually high number upon joining the White Sox as a free agent in 1981, reversing the No. 27 he had donned as a member of the Red Sox.

96—Bill Voiselle: Upon being traded to the Braves in 1947, sported the number of his hometown: Ninety Six, South Carolina.

Basketball

00—Robert Parish: The "Chief." Celtic great was nine-time All-Star, won four NBA titles, and in 1997 became the oldest player to appear in an NBA game (at age 43).

3—Allen Iverson: The diminutive shooting guard has shown the ability to dominate a big-man's sport, with an MVP trophy and a career scoring average of 28 points per game.

6—Bill Russell: Won 11 NBA titles during 13-year career with Celtics (1956-69) and considered among the greatest players and defensive centers in league history.

6—Julius Erving: This doctor didn't make house calls, but he breathed new life into the NBA in the 1970s.

8/24—Kobe Bryant: Lakers shooting guard who "three-peated" with Shaq and hung 81 points on the scoreboard in a single game, second only to Wilt Chamberlain.

11—Isiah Thomas: One of the game's great point guards who was a 12-time All-Star and won two NBA championships with the Pistons.

12—John Stockton: All-time NBA leader in assists and steals.

13—Wilt Chamberlain: Most dominant offensive force in NBA history once averaged 50.4 points per game for an entire season.

14—Bob Cousy: Redefined the point guard position while leading the NBA in assists for eight straight years and was part of six title teams with the Celtics.

14/1—Oscar Robertson: Twelve-time All-Star is the only player in NBA history to average a triple-double for an entire season.

19—Willis Reed: In 1969-70 won All-Star Game MVP, regular season MVP, and playoff MVP while helping the Knicks to their first NBA championship.

21—Tim Duncan: All-tools frontcourt player admired for his consistency and demeanor, who three times has been named MVP of the NBA Finals while leading the Spurs to the title.

23/45—Michael Jordan: All he ever did was win five MVP awards, 10 scoring titles, reach the All-Defensive team nine times, and help the Bulls to six NBA titles.

24—Bill Bradley: Princeton grad, Rhodes Scholar, United States senator, and a 10-year NBA pro who is in the Basketball Hall of Fame.

31—Reggie Miller: The NBA's career leader in three-pointers who once nailed a three-point shot in 58 consecutive games.

32—Earvin "Magic" Johnson: At 6'9", could play any position on the court and won league MVP honors three times while leading the Lakers to five NBA championships.

32—Karl Malone: Sculpted power forward played 19 NBA seasons and was a 14-time All-Star and two-time MVP who retired as league's second all-time leading scorer.

32—Shaquille O'Neal: The 7'1", 325-pound giant has won four NBA championships with the Lakers and Heat, twice led the league in scoring, and was league's 1999-2000 MVP.

33—Kareem Abdul-Jabbar: NBA's all-time scoring leader known for his "Sky Hook" won MVP award six times and was part of six NBA title teams with the Bucks and Lakers.

33—Larry Bird: Skilled, creative, smart, and an intense competitor, he won MVP honors three times and helped the Celtics to a trio of NBA Championships.

41—Wes Unseld: At 6'7", an undersized center who stymied opponents with his intensity and physical play, and won NBA's MVP and Rookie of Year honors in 1968-69.

44—George Gervin: The "Ice Man" won four NBA scoring titles and averaged 26.2 points per game for his NBA career.

44—Jerry West: Classic playmaker used in the NBA's silhouette logo averaged 27.0 points per game for his career and scored at an even better 29.1 points-per-game clip in 153 playoff appearances.

50—David Robinson: Ten-time All-Star won scoring, rebounding, and blocked-shot titles during his career and was part of two NBA title teams with the Spurs.

76—Shawn Bradley: Beanpole center wore a number that represented his height and his first NBA team (Philadelphia 76ers).

99—George Mikan: The game's first dominant big man won five league titles with the Lakers and was the first NBA player to score 10,000 career points.

Football

00—Jim Otto: Fifteen-year Raiders veteran who was the only All-League center in the history of the American Football League.

0—George Plimpton: Famed writer donned this number while playing in a preseason game for the Lions as part of the research for his classic sports book *Paper Lion*.

12—Tom Brady: Patriots signal caller won three Super Bowl rings—and was twice the game's MVP—in his first five years in the NFL.

12—Joe Namath: The man who "guaranteed" a Jets win in Super Bowl III became the first player to throw for 4,000 yards in a single season.

13—Dan Marino: The greatest passer in NFL history threw for 61,000 yards and had 420 touchdowns in his 17-year career with the Dolphins.

14—Otto Graham: Either won a division or league title in each of his 10 pro seasons and had three passing touchdowns and three rushing touchdowns in the Browns' 1954 NFL Championship Game win.

16—Joe Montana: The prototype West Coast quarterback is the only three-time Super Bowl MVP and was never intercepted in his four Super Bowl appearances.

18—Peyton Manning: Capped 2006 season by being named Super Bowl XLI MVP after setting an NFL record by throwing for more than 4,000 yards for the seventh time in his career.

19—Johnny Unitas: Three-time NFL Player of the Year and, until Peyton Manning came along, held an NFL record by throwing a touchdown pass in 47 straight games.

20—Barry Sanders: First player in NFL history to rush for 1,000 yards in each of his first 10 seasons and posted 14 straight 100-yard games in 1997.

21—LaDainian Tomlinson: Running back set an NFL mark with 31 touchdowns during the 2006 season, including a five-game span where he scored 16 times.

30—Bill Willis: Reintegrated pro football when he signed with the AFL's Cleveland Browns in 1946, one year before Jackie Robinson broke baseball's color barrier.

32—Jim Brown: The game's most prolific running back averaged 5.2 yards per carry and 104.3 rushing yards per game for his career.

32—O.J. Simpson: Became the NFL's first 2,000-yard rusher when he erupted for 2,003 yards with the Bills in 1973.

33—Sammy Baugh: Finished as NFL's passing, punting, and interception leader in 1943. Now top that!

34—Earl Campbell: NFL Player of the Year, rushing champion, All-Pro, and Pro Bowl selection for three straight years between 1978 and 1980, and had four 200-yard rushing efforts during the 1980 season.

34—Walter Payton: Retired in 1987 as the NFL's all-time rushing leader with 16,726 yards and is still ranked by some as the greatest running back to play the game.

41—Brian Piccolo: 1960s Bears running back whose tragic battle with cancer was immortalized in the movie *Brian's Song*.

51—Dick Butkus: Eight-time Pro Bowl selection whose speed, instincts, and strength defined the middle linebacker position in the 1960s and '70s.

56—Lawrence Taylor: Two-time Super Bowl champ revolutionized defense and refined the linebacker position.

60—Chuck Bednarik: The last of pro football's 60-minute men, he played center and linebacker on the Eagles' 1960 NFL title team.

70—Art Donovan: Hall of Fame defensive tackle who became famous to younger generations for his offbeat appearances on *Late Night with David Letterman*.

73—John Hannah: All-Pro offensive guard for 10 straight seasons and may be the best to ever play the game at his position.

74—Bruce Matthews: Offensive lineman and 2007 Pro Football Hall of Fame inductee is co-holder of the league record with 14 Pro Bowl selections.

76—Lou Groza: "The Toe" was an offensive guard and place-kicker for the Browns who played 21 seasons and reached nine NFL title games.

85—Jack Youngblood: Seven-time Pro Bowl defensive end proved as tough as he was good by playing the entire 1979 NFL playoffs with a broken left leg.

88—Alan Page: Defensive tackle on the Vikings' Purple People Eaters defense appeared in 236 straight games and went on to became a justice on the Minnesota Supreme Court.

92—Reggie White: The late "Minister of Defense" retired with a since-broken NFL-record 198 sacks in his 16-year career.

Ice Hockey

1—Bernie Parent: Backstopped Flyers to two Stanley Cup titles in the early 1970s and became the first hockey player to appear on the cover of *Time* magazine.

1—Jacques Plante: Longtime netminder popularized the goalie's mask and won Vezina Trophy as NHL's top goalie a record seven times.

2—Al MacInnis: Owner of the most lethal slap shot in hockey history and was selected to 15 All-Star Games.

4—Bobby Orr*: See pg. 78.

6—Irvine "Ace" Bailey: 1928-29 league scoring leader whose career was cut short by a vicious hit from Boston's Eddie Shore and then became first NHL player to have his number retired.

7—Paul Coffey: The quintessential offensive defenseman scored 396 career goals and once had eight points in a game.

7—Phil Esposito: First NHL player to reach 100 points in a season, with 126 for the Bruins in 1968-69, and finished his career with 717 career goals.

9—Gordie Howe: Forward's glorious career spanned from 1945 to 1980—that's six decades, you know—playing nearly 2,200 games while scoring 801 goals.

9—Bobby Hull: Legendary offensive force tallied 913 goals in his career and was twice named NHL Most Valuable Player and WHA Most Valuable Player.

9—Maurice Richard: "The Rocket" was the first player to score 50 goals in 50 games and played for eight Stanley Cup-winning teams.

10—Guy Lafleur: Smooth-skating forward was three-time scoring leader and two-time MVP who starred for five Stanley Cup championship teams.

11—Mark Messier: His amazing 25-year NHL career saw him amass 1,887 points, claim two MVP awards, appear in 15 All-Star Games, and win six Stanley Cup titles.

16—Bobby Clarke: Three-time league MVP overcame diabetes to play pro hockey and was the face of the Flyers' Broad Street Bullies in the 1970s.

19—Steve Yzerman: Among the top scorers in NHL history (1,755 points) but also a tremendous defensive player who helped the Red Wings capture a trio of Stanley Cup titles.

21—Stan Mikita: The possessor of hockey's first great slap shot during the 1960s, he finished with 541 goals and was the NHL scoring leader on four occasions.

29—Ken Dryden: Game's top goalie of the 1970s played in just 397 games but still won the Vezina Trophy five times, recorded 46 shutouts, and had a career 2.24 goals against average.

33—Patrick Roy: Arguably the greatest goalie of all time, he won a league-record 551 regular season games and another 151 in the playoffs.

66-Mario Lemieux: A six-time NHL scoring leader who came back to play after treatment for Hodgkin's lymphoma, he selected his number in honor of Wayne Gretzky.

68—Jaromir Jagr: Holder of record for points in a season by a right wing (149), he chose his number in tribute to his grandfather, who died in prison during the Soviet Union's 1968 invasion of his native Czechoslovakia.

77—Ray Bourque: Five-time Norris Trophy winner and all-time leading scorer among defensemen (1,579), he switched from his No. 7 when the Bruins honored Phil Esposito.

87—Sidney Crosby: The NHL's next great player who in 2005-06, at age 19, became the youngest player in league history to amass 100 points in a season.

89—Alexander Mogilny: This skilled Russian tallied 473 career goals and chose his number to reflect the year he defected from the Soviet Union.

99—Wayne Gretzky: The greatest offensive force in the history of the game originally picked out his number as a tribute to Gordie Howe.

Other

3—Dale Earnhardt (NASCAR)*: See pg. 76.

6—Brandi Chastain (Soccer): Team USA star forever famous for her penalty-kick goal against China—and post-game removal of her jersey—in gold-medal game at the 1999 Women's World Cup.

10—Diego Maradona (Soccer): Among the greatest and most controversial soccer stars in history, scored five goals and had five assists in leading Argentina to the 1986 World Cup.

10—Pelé (Soccer): Member of three World Cup Championship teams with Brazil and was signed by New York's Cosmos in the 1970s to help popularize soccer in America.

10—Mia Hamm (Soccer): Member of four NCAA title teams at North Carolina, won two Olympic gold medals, was part of the 1999 World Cup, and retired in 2004 with a record 158 goals in international competition. And she's married to Nomar Garciaparra.

21—Cale Yarborough (NASCAR): Four-time Daytona 500 winner was also the first to win three straight Nextel Cup championships.

24—Jeff Gordon (NASCAR): Four-time Nextel Cup champion has been responsible for moving auto racing into America's mainstream.

43—Richard Petty (NASCAR): Legendary driver captured 200 races, won seven NASCAR championships, and is among the most popular drivers in history.

50W—Rosie Ruiz (Boston Marathon): Number worn by infamous "winner" of women's 1980 Boston Marathon who was stripped of her crown after being accused of entering race in the final mile.

61—Johnny Kelly (Boston Marathon): Two-time Boston Marathon champion had this number retired in honor of the 61 times he ran the race, the last coming in 1992 at age 84.

Digital Display

While other sports teams may have tinkered with using uniform numbers previously—reports have minor league baseball's Reading Red Roses putting them on players in 1907—it was the New York Yankees that made numerical identification a permanent fixture. In January 1929, the Yankees announced they would adopt player numbers for that season and were almost immediately followed by the Cleveland Indians (who had experimented with numbers in 1916 and 1917). On April 16, 1929, the Yankees took the field in uniform numbers, assigning them to players based on their position in the batting order, hence Babe Ruth wore No. 3 and Lou Gehrig wore No. 4. Within three years the concept became commonplace and spread to other sports. Staving off the inevitable, the old-school Philadelphia Athletics, led by suit-wearing manager Connie Mack, didn't join the numbers game until 1937.

This chapter covers some intriguing numbers from history. Pat Riley was smart enough to put a patent on the phrase "three-peat." Remember when Moses Malone predicted his Sixers would run away in the playoffs with three straight sweeps? His chant of four-four-four was memorable and almost right, but not quite. I tried to recruit Moses, and he is still a person I consider to be near and dear to me and my family. I love talking to him whenever I see him.

The Fab Five of Michigan was a team I enjoyed watching. Chris Webber, Juwan Howard, Jalen Rose, Ray Jackson, and Jimmy King helped Steve Fisher earn a trip to the national title game. I don't know if we will ever see a more talented freshmen group ever. Yes, some teams will have three and maybe even four diaper dandies in the starting lineup. But all five, like the Wolverines did, and then seeing them making a serious run through the tournament...that was a very special group. It is sad to know that Chris Webber's involvement in the scandal with booster Ed Martin was costly. Michigan's NCAA tournament appearances with the Fab Five were vacated by the NCAA. There was a black mark put on the school due to the infractions.

The number 46 stands out because that signified the Bears defense that dominated the Patriots in the Super Bowl. Mike Ditka and Buddy Ryan had an awesome unit that impressed many. Guys like Mike Singletary, Dan Hampton, and Steve McMichael were outstanding. This may have been the best defensive squad in NFL history.

THE ONE AND ONLY

Singulary Special Numbers from Our Sporting Past

1/8

Eddie Gaedel

A PINT-SIZED PINCH HITTER WAS A **BIG HIT** FOR THE ST. LOUIS BROWNS.

NUMBELIEVABLE

Who needs Hollywood? Eddie Gaedel had his walk of fame at St. Louis's Sportsman's Park.

On August 19, 1951, with 18,369 wildly amused fans cheering him on, the 3'7" Gaedel drew perhaps the most memorable walk in the history of Major League Baseball.

His appearance was the brainchild of Browns owner Bill Veeck, the notorious promoter who would later bring us the exploding scoreboard and "Disco Demolition Night." Looking to attract a big crowd for an otherwise insignificant Sunday doubleheader between his eighth-place team and the fifth-place Detroit Tigers, Veeck promised a "Festival of Surprises" for fans in attendance.

The day's shenanigans included jugglers, a band conducted by pitching great Satchel Paige, an appearance by baseball clown prince Max Patkin, and a giant papier-mâché cake from which Gaedel leaped out between games. Yet the biggest—no, make that smallest—surprise was still to come.

In the first inning of game two, St. Louis lead-off hitter and starting right fielder Frank Saucier was called back from the batter's box for a pinch-hitter. Sent up in his place was the pint-sized Gaedel, wearing a uniform borrowed from the Browns' nine-year-old batboy with the number ⅛ emblazoned on the back.

Home plate umpire Ed Hurley initially challenged the move. But when St. Louis manager Zack Taylor produced a copy of Gaedel's signed contract—paying him $100 per game—the umpire relented.

Veeck's instructions were clear: don't swing. In his 1962 autobiography, *Veeck—As in Wreck*, he repeated what he had told Gaedel. "Eddie, I'm going to be up on the roof with a high-powered rifle watching every move you make. If you so much as look as if you're going to swing, I'm going to shoot you dead." There was no need to worry. Gaedel carried with him a toy bat and stood as far away from the plate as he could.

Detroit pitcher Bob Cain initially attempted to throw a strike, but with Gaedel's strike zone measuring a scant one-and-one-half inches, it proved impossible. After two serious pitches, a bemused Cain lobbed the next two high over Gaedel's head for a walk. Twice on his way to first, Gaedel stopped to take a bow; upon reaching the bag, he was replaced by pinch runner Jim Delsing.

Back in the dugout, Saucier kidded Gaedel about his elongated trot to first base. Gaedel responded, "Man, I felt like Babe Root [Ruth]," Saucier told ESPN.com's Darren Rovell.

While the promotion garnered nationwide attention, the story didn't end well. The Browns lost the game, 6-2, and American League commissioner Will Harridge voided Gaedel's contract the next day. While Gaedel appeared in several more Veeck promotions over the years, a heart attack took his life at the age of 36.

But for one day, a walk had made little Eddie Gaedel baseball's biggest star.

THE SPRITE OF ST. LOUIS By pinch-hitting for the Browns in a 1951 game against the Tigers, 3'7" Eddie Gaedel became the shortest player to appear in a major league game.

THREE-PEAT

PAT RILEY OWNS THE PHRASE THAT PAYS.

Pat Riley

It doesn't seem scientifically possible, but Pat Riley just might be slicker than his hair.

Not only has the dapper former player, executive, and broadcaster coached two separate franchises to NBA titles—his 2005-06 Miami Heat squad and the Los Angeles Lakers in the glory days of "Showtime"—but Mr. Riley also found a way to profit even when his rival, then-Chicago Bulls coach Phil Jackson, made history.

He trademarked the word "three-peat." Linguistically speaking, that's a portmanteau—a melding of two separate words to create a new one, a la "brunch."

Speaking of champagne, in the fall of 1988 Riley's Lakers came into the season as two-time defending NBA champions, gunning for their third straight title. Guard Byron Scott stated that the team's goal was to "three-peat," coining a phrase that would wind up putting a lot of coin in Riley's well-tailored pockets. In November of that year, Riles & Co., the coach's company, submitted an application (U.S. Registration number 1552980) for the use of "three-peat" on shirts, jackets, and hats. This marked one of the only known times in hoop history that a coach scored, and his player (Scott) got the assist.

When the Lakers reached the NBA Finals for the third time, it seemed like the prescient coach was ready to cash in. However, the "Bad Boy" Detroit Pistons had other ideas, with Isiah Thomas and Joe Dumars stomping the Lakers, taking the Larry O'Brien trophy, and presumably keeping Riley's triplicate souvenirs in deep storage.

However, since the use of "three-peat" was not trademarked exclusively in linkage with the Lakers, a shift in power in the NBA gave Riley his golden opportunity four years later. With Michael Jordan leading the Chicago Bulls to championships in 1991, 1992, and 1993, it was a "three-peat" accompli. Ironically, in order to add one more back- to their back-to-back titles in 1993, the Bulls first had to roar past the Riley-coached New York Knicks in the Eastern Conference Finals. With an estimated 5 percent royalties on any licensed item bearing the "3" word, at least Riley was able to rake in a consolation prize of an estimated $300,000.

Los Angeles finally did experience a three-peat in the NBA, but once again Jackson was at the helm, as the Lakers took championships in 2000, 2001, and 2002. The town was gearing up for another a few years later when the USC Trojans looked like they might be closing in on their third straight national football championship. Local fan Kyle Bunch started vending "Three-Pete" T-shirts, in honor of USC coach Pete Carroll, but he was served with a cease-and-desist order and stopped selling the shirts rather than pay the royalty.

"It's like going out there and picking up a penny on the ground," said Riley about the three-peat windfall, which he says has mostly been given to charity. "It's sort of been an interesting phenomenon," he added. "I found out that if I were ever an entrepreneurial man, I could have made some [money] in my life."

Did I Stutter?

Famous Three-Peats (and Beyond) in Pro Sports History:

Basketball
Minneapolis Lakers 1952-54

Boston Celtics 1959-66 (technically an eight-peat)

Chicago Bulls 1991-93; 1996-98

Los Angeles Lakers 2000-02

Football
Green Bay Packers 1929-31; 1965-67

Hockey
Toronto Maple Leafs 1947-49; 1962-64

Montreal Canadiens 1956-60; 1976-79

New York Islanders 1980-83

Baseball
New York Yankees 1936-39; 1949-53; 1998-2000

Oakland Athletics 1972-74

DON'T YA RILE 'EM Dapper Lakers coach Pat Riley was gagged by his 1989 NBA championship team at their celebration so he wouldn't promise a three-peat.

MOSES MALONE IMPARTED A SWEEPING PREDICTION FOR THE 76ERS.

4-4-4

Moses Malone

"Fo'-fo'-fo'."

The Gettysburg Address of NBA smack-talk, this was the infamous, phonetically truncated utterance of Philadelphia 76ers center Moses Malone when asked to predict how his team would fare in the 1983 playoffs. The soon-to-be three-time MVP was a man on a mission, boldly prognosticating an unprecedented three-tiered sweep for Philly.

Going into the regular season, Philadelphia owner Harold Katz was tired of losing in the postseason to the rival Boston Celtics and Los Angeles Lakers, so he pulled off a whopper of a move. The Sixers acquired the 6'10", 265-pound Malone from the Houston Rockets in a sign-and-trade deal for Caldwell Jones, a first-round draft pick, and a substantial new contract for Moses. The acquisition made the cover of *Sports Illustrated* and changed the balance of power in the league.

Malone was added to an already formidable lineup that included another future Hall of Famer in team captain Julius Erving, the deadly backcourt of Maurice Cheeks and Andrew Toney, plus supersub Bobby Jones (named the winner of the NBA's first Sixth Man Award that year). After storming through the regular season with a 65-17 mark, the team was stacked and hungry for more. Malone's comment didn't even cause a stir on his own team.

"It was that Malone confidence," Jones explained. "It was confidence that he had backed up before with his actions." Clearly, coach Billy Cunningham's squad was not an underdog heading into the postseason.

However, let the record show that the blunt Malone didn't exactly lack for confidence when he was the underdog. Two years prior Moses had taken an undermanned and sub-.500 Houston Rockets team onto his broad shoulders and almost to the "Promised Land." They knocked off the defending champion Lakers in the first round and roared all the way into the NBA Finals versus a Boston Celtics squad featuring the likes of Larry Bird, Kevin McHale and Robert Parish. Whether it was a motivational ploy or simply a lot of blarney, Malone called the Celtics "chumps" and claimed that "me and four guys from Petersburg [Virginia, his hometown]" could beat the powerhouse team. Maybe so, but the Rockets sure didn't. Still, it took the Celtics six games to win the championship.

But now, back to our fo'. Malone, Dr. J, and crew swept the Knicks in their first playoff series and had Milwaukee down 3-0 before Moses's words finally rang hollow. The Bucks pulled out a 100-94 victory in Game 4 of the Eastern Conference Finals, but Philly still advanced in five.

The Sixers then resoundingly exorcised ghosts of past Finals lost to the "Showtime" Los Angeles Lakers in 1980 and '82 with a clean sweep of a hobbled Lakers team in the Finals. Malone outrebounded Kareem Abdul-Jabbar, 72-30, in the four-game series, taking home the Finals MVP trophy to go along with his regular-season hardware, and Dr. J finally had his first NBA title.

Although Moses's words weren't quite prophesy, his team finished with a record of 12-1, which still stands as the most dominant run in NBA playoff history. Otherwise known as "Fo'-fi'-fo."

AND HE WALKED THE WALK
Sixers center Moses Malone predicted three straight sweeps for his team in the 1983 NBA playoffs—he missed by just one game, but Philly still captured its first title in 16 years.

Fab 5

Michigan Basketball

There are many ways to view the legacy of college basketball's most famous recruiting class ever, the University of Michigan's so-called "Fab 5": pioneering freshmen, stylish and mature beyond their years; just another collection of overhyped, underachieving superstars; or, more darkly, as symbols of everything that's wrong with modern-day big-time college athletics.

The story began when Juwan Howard, Ray Jackson, Jimmy King, Jalen Rose, and Chris Webber arrived in Ann Arbor in the fall of 1991 with blue-chip pedigrees, sky-high expectations, and Beatles-esque hype. It was an age when ESPN and sports media in general were exploding into pop culture and were ravenous for fresh new poster boys.

Enter the Fab 5. (Note to Pat Riley: the "Quintessential Quintet" is still there for the taking.)

Brimming with skill, confidence, and pizzazz, this close-knit group of basketball wunderkinds was supposed to shake up the college basketball world like a snow globe. Blizzard accomplished.

Sporting renegade black athletic socks, untucked long jerseys, and a fluid, fast-paced game that showcased their athleticism and impressive ballhandling skills, the Fab 5 instantaneously reversed the downward trend of Coach Steve Fisher's program. Webber, Howard, and Rose quickly established themselves as stars—as they later did in the NBA—and the Fab 5 completed their inaugural season with a gaudy record of 25 wins against 9 losses, improving markedly on the previous year's listless 14-15 finish.

The versatile King and Jackson worked their way into the starting lineup by midseason, which enabled the Fab 5 to make history by being the first and only starting five of freshmen to carry a team all the way to the Final Four.

"From what the media has told me and from what I can see, we've never had freshmen playing like this in the history of college basketball," displaced starter James Voskuil said. "So yeah, it's a lot of media hype, but they're worth it."

Of course, to put this feat into proper context, it should be noted that college freshmen weren't eligible to play on varsity squads until 1972-73. But still, it seems unlikely that such a kiddie-coup would have been accomplished in the era when players stayed in school throughout all four years of their eligibility. The closest challenging predecessor probably would've been when young Lew Alcindor led a UCLA graduating class that boasted four sophomore starters on the championship team of 1967.

Although the Fab 5 ended their season absorbing a 20-point drubbing by defending champion Duke in the NCAA title game, even their conquerors were impressed. "They were phenomenal in the first half, but our experience with Grant Hill, Bobby Hurley, and Christian Laettner won out," said Tommy Amaker, then a Duke assistant coach and later the head man at Michigan.

The Fab 5 also boosted more than morale back on campus—athletic royalties went from $2 million in 1990, the year before the five arrived, to $4.4 million in 1992.

The next season would be the last for the full complement of the Fab 5, ending with another fruitless trip to the championship game. In this one, a much tighter game against North Carolina, the exquisitely talented Webber, a 6'9" big man with a pure jump shot and the generous heart of a point guard, made a youthful crunch-time mistake—signaling for a timeout in the closing seconds when Michigan had none left, and thus drawing a technical foul. The error effectively ended the game.

It was Webber's last game as a collegian. He entered the NBA draft after his sophomore season, ending the group's whirlwind, twice-shy run.

"There will never be a freshman class to do that again," Webber said after the loss to Duke in that first championship game. He meant the on-court achievements, but the rest of it applies, too.

GET FRESH CREW Jalen Rose, Chris Webber, and the rest of the Fab 5 made college hoop history by reaching the NCAA final with an all-freshman starting unit.

6'4 3/4"

Charles Barkley

Charles Barkley barreled out of Auburn University with a large nickname, The Round Mound of Rebound, and a game to match. In a sport where long and lithe players are considered imperative for success, the Chuckster was a pleasingly plump anomaly.

"Charles Barkley is unique with his body frame, with his structure, with his jumping ability," rival coach Pat Riley once said. "The whole thing is unique, and that's why he is truly great."

Well known for being brutally candid and perhaps cocky, even the young Barkley didn't foresee greatness for himself in the pro ranks. "When I got drafted, I knew I had a God-given ability to rebound," he said. "But I never averaged more than 14 points a game in college. So I was just hoping I could score 10 points and get 10 rebounds a game for a few years and make some money to take care of my family."

Can we super-size those goals for you, Mr. Barkley? By force of will, and by taking advantage of impressive natural gifts that were sometimes cloaked by calories, he turned into an NBA MVP (1993), an 11-time All-Star, and the shortest rebounding champion in NBA history. The official records may have listed him at 6'6", but he has copped to being more in the vicinity of 6'4¾", and game photos of him standing next to other players, such as 6'6" buddy Michael Jordan, seem to bear this claim out.

In just his third season in the league, Barkley topped all rebounders, hauling down 14.6 per game. The previous two champions had been centers—his Philadelphia mentor, the 6'10" Moses Malone, and 6'11" Bill Laimbeer. "Any knucklehead can score," Barkley famously once said. "It takes brains to rebound." Of course, when it came to boxing out, Barkley admittedly had more to work with. His wife Maureen once said that his rear end is "the size of New Jersey."

Usually giving up three or more inches in height to the players he defended, Barkley made up for it by being the Tasmanian Devil on Twinkies. "A game for Charles is a passionate experience," said Matt Guokas, Barkley's one-time coach with the Philadelphia 76ers. "I've never seen anyone so ferocious in wanting to prove he's better than his opponent."

Just like Jordan, Barkley had been cut from his high school basketball team. But he worked doggedly, including leaping drills that required propelling his hefty frame (at times approaching 300 pounds in college) over a 4-foot chainlink fence. He eventually left most of his body fat behind, but he remained big-boned and was listed at 252 pounds for the stretch run of his amazing career.

He never won an NBA title, but it certainly wasn't for lack of effort. Bill Lyon of *The Philadelphia Inquirer* likened Barkley to "an 18-wheeler roaring down a steep grade." One of his ferocious dunks knocked a 2,200-pound basket support off line by about six inches. He averaged at least 10 boards a game for 15 of his 16 NBA seasons.

After eight tumultuous seasons in Philadelphia, Barkley found new life when he was traded to the Phoenix Suns. Teamed up with Kevin Johnson and Dan Majerle, he led them to the NBA Finals in 1993, but despite Barkley's extraordinary efforts, Jordan and the Bulls were not to be denied.

"He gets rebounds that no one ever has gotten here," Phoenix executive Cotton Fitzsimmons said. "How does he do it? There simply aren't guys that size who play pro basketball. They all have become linebackers somewhere."

Even toward the end, when his knees and back were going, the indefatigable Barkley made one last run at a championship when he teamed up with two other aging All-Stars, Hakeem Olajuwon and Clyde Drexler, in Houston. There were whispers that Barkley was running on fumes. In his first game in a Houston uniform in November 1996, he grabbed 33 rebounds, a career high, with an astonishing 25 in the first half. Fume that.

There are only four players in NBA history who have 20,000 points, 10,000 rebounds, and 4,000 assists in a career—Wilt Chamberlain, Kareem Abdul-Jabbar, Karl Malone, and Barkley (who finished with 23,752 points, 12,546 rebounds, and 4,215 assists). The first two are 7-footers, and Malone is 6'9".

He may have been a 6'4¾" power forward, but he was never short on words, nor on effort.

(photo courtesy Getty Images)

Island Green at TPC Sawgrass

Golf's toughest hole? Not by a long shot. But the most nerve-wracking? Absolutely.

It's the picturesque par-3 17th hole at TPC Sawgrass, both loved and loathed for its intimidating "Island Green." Normally, a 132-yard hole that rarely requires more than a wedge would elicit yawns from spectators and birdies from golfers, but fans and TV cameras unfailingly flock to this location, for there may not be another tee shot on tour that rattles the game's best like this one.

Chalk it up to a melding of conditions, design, and placement. First, PGA players must deal with the surly winds that rush through northern Florida in the early spring, gusts that often arise from a calm and are eager to blow a lofted golf ball off course. Then comes the tee shot's simple win or lose outcome: it's either on (the green) or it's in (the water). Now pile on the fact it's the next-to-last hole in one of the game's most challenging finishes in a tournament—The Players Championship, frequently labeled golf's fifth major—and you've got pressure that could make Roy "Tin Cup" McAvoy feel a lump in his throat.

"There are 361 days a year when it's a very easy hole," 1988 PGA champion Jeff Sluman explained to *Florida Times Union* writer Gary Smits. "In practice rounds, you wonder how you can miss the green. [But] Thursday through Sunday, the week of The Players [Championship], it's one of the most difficult shots you can face."

In 1998 Len Mattiace came to the 17th tee on Sunday trailing leader Justin Leonard by one shot. He then knocked two balls into the water and took a quintuple-bogey 8. Tom Watson fell out of contention with a fourth-round snowman of his own in 1990. Yet those scores were three strokes better than what Robert Gamez carded during 1990's third round; Gamez deposited four shots into the drink and limped away with an 11. At least he had already made the cut.

"I'm going to be honest...there's not much about that day I remember," Gamez told Smits. "I kept hitting shots and they kept going into the water. It's a good hole. I just had a very bad day."

It even gets into the head of those who consistently conquered it.

"I once stood on the 17th tee with a 6-shot lead and was still worried about getting it across the water. I knew if I put one in the drink, I might put 10 in. It's one of those feelings," maintained Australian Steve Elkington—a two-time TPC Sawgrass winner—in an interview with *Golf World*'s Ron Whitten.

If golfers believe the hole was always intended to be a cruel joke inflicted upon them by course designer Pete Dye, they are mistaken. It came about as a matter of necessity. Original plans placed a water hazard only along the right side, but as construction began on the course—located in swampy lands outside Jacksonville, Florida—a pocket of highly desired sand was unearthed in front of the 17th green.

"We needed good, quality sand for developing the fairways," revealed then-PGA Commissioner Dean Beman to pgatour.com's Mark Cubbedge. "As the holes started developing, we needed more and more sand, and that's where the good sand was. So that's were the lake is."

Dye's wife, Alice, stared at the mini-canyon and suggested an island green. And so one was built—90 feet deep and 87 feet wide, accompanied only by a smallish potbelly sand trap along the right side. The green narrows as it goes away from the tee, and the back right side—a frequent Sunday pin location—sits a foot lower than the main part of the green. The hole didn't yield its first hole-in-one until the tournament's fifth year, when Brad Fabel aced his shot in the opening round of the 1986 TPC, and course officials estimate 100,000 balls annually sink into the waters surrounding the green.

In competition, the hole is set up perfectly. It comes right after a risk-reward, 497-yard par-5 and is followed by the number one-ranked hole on the Stadium Course, a 440-yard par-4 that rotates left with water anchoring the left side from tee to green. Dye's design provides brilliant theater, creating a challenge that prevents a final-round leader from shifting his game into cruise control...even if he knows how to control his nerves.

MULLIGAN'S ISLAND? The 17th hole at TPC Sawgrass has mystified many a golfer over the years.

(photo courtesy Getty Images)

Defense

"DA BEARS" DOMINATED BECAUSE OF BUDDY RYAN'S INNOVATIVE DEFENSE.

This went way beyond respect. It was surrender. Upon watching Buddy Ryan's "46" defense decimate one opponent after another during the Bears' march to the Super Bowl XX title, the NFL's greatest offensive minds retreated en masse. Before their very eyes—and in practically a single season—the game of football had changed.

In Ryan's unique system, the defense was the aggressor. It attacked with eight defenders in the box, overwhelming offensive lines, unnerving quarterbacks, and eating up runners before they could find the line of scrimmage.

This wasn't something he dreamed up overnight. Ryan had worked as a defensive assistant on the Jets' Super Bowl III title team that stymied the heavily favored Colts. He then went to Minnesota, teaming with Neill Armstrong to keep the Vikings' Purple People Eaters defense among the NFL's elite through the mid-1970s. When Armstrong was named the Bears' head coach in 1978, he brought Ryan along as his defensive coordinator. As Ryan's thinking

evolved and the players around him matured, he began constructing a defense that many still rate the best the league has ever known.

"When I was coaching with the Jets, I used to listen to [head coach] Weeb [Ewbank] say, 'The most important job for the offense was to protect the quarterback,'" Ryan told *The Boston Globe* in 1986. "From that, I concluded that the most important job of the defense is to get to the quarterback. I believe if a quarterback is secure, eventually he will find his man. So we rush as many men as it takes to make him feel insecure."

The Bears' defense took its name from the uniform number of defensive back Doug Plank. In Ryan's original scheme, Plank—a pulverizing hitter who spent eight years in the league before retiring in 1982—would move up from his safety spot to become an extra linebacker, where he either blitzed himself or filled the spot vacated by another blitzer.

"We try to create situations where the offensive line has to lot to think about," said Ryan in another *Globe* interview. "When we do, they can't be aggressive. We muss up their blocking schemes."

By 1985 the formation was being fronted by a pair of future Hall of Famers, middle linebacker Mike Singletary and defensive end Dan Hampton. But the Bears' defensive talent pool ran deep, too...with defensive end Richard Dent (who was named Super Bowl XX MVP), defensive tackles Steve McMichael and William Perry, linebackers Otis Wilson and Wilber Marshall, cornerback Leslie Frazier, and free safety Gary Fencik. The scary part is that two of the team's top players from 1984—linebacker Al Harris and strong safety Todd Bell—held out the entire championship season in contract disputes.

Haunted by a 23-0 loss to the 49ers in the previous year's NFC Championship Game, the Bears raised their play to an almost unfathomable level. They boasted the league's top-ranked defense in both yards allowed and points allowed, collected 64 sacks (including 17 by Dent), and permitted more than 10 points just five times in 19 games spanning the regular season and playoffs.

They did stumble once, on a raucous Monday night in Miami after starting the year 12-0. The Dolphins were the defending AFC champs and on their way to a fourth straight AFC East title. They were also defending history, with members of their '72 squad—the only team to roll through an entire NFL season undefeated—watching from the sidelines.

"Everyone gave them [Chicago] a chance of going undefeated and winning it all," recalled Miami wide receiver Nat Moore in a 2002 interview with ABC Sports Online editor Mike Diegnan. "It was great offense against great defense, and that particular night, great offense won."

While there would be no perfection, the Bears and their defense quickly rebounded. Chicago won its final three regular season games to finish 15-1 and then shut out the Giants and Rams in the NFC playoffs. And to call their Super Bowl XX performance against the Patriots dominant would be grossly understating it. New England's starting quarterback, Tony Eason, didn't complete a pass and was replaced in the second quarter while leading rusher Tony Collins amassed four yards. Time of possession favored Chicago by nearly 20 minutes. After yielding an early field goal, the Bears erupted for 44 straight points while rolling to a 46-10 victory.

In a break from tradition, both head coach Mike Ditka and Ryan were carried off the Superdome field on the shoulders of their players. It was a final salute for Ryan, who was on his way to Philadelphia to become that team's head coach.

Akebono

Over the long and storied tradition of the Japanese sport of Sumo, in the 300 years leading up to 1993, there had been only 63 *yokozuna*, or grand champions. Obviously, this ultimate rank in this heavyweight world is not awarded lightly. So it was somewhat of a shock to the system, and a whole nation, when the 64th was crowned—a *gaijin* (outside person) from Hawaii. He was born Chad Rowan, but came to be known as Akebono.

A towering 6'8", he was much taller than the traditional *rikishi* (sumo wrestler) and tipped the scales somewhere around 500 pounds for most of his career. Beating the odds to attain *yokozuna* status (only one out of 336 even make the pro sumo cut in the first place) was a far cry from Akebono's early days in Japan, when the gigantic man had a rocky transition into this unforgiving sport that truly is a way of life.

Living in cramped stable housing, training for hours a day, doing menial work, and serving his elders without fail took quite a toll. After all, this was a laid-back former high school basket-ball player who had earlier envisioned a long and leisurely life relaxing on the beaches of his native state. "I cried every night," he said. "I thought that I was a man but I found out that I was a baby."

As his skills developed, and he adjusted to the spartan sumo culture, the quietly competitive Akebono started to blossom. *Rikishi* advance up the ranks if they consistently win more than half of the 15 bouts they have in each *basho* (tournament). After three years of middling success, the long-legged Akebono stepped up his game, overcoming his top-heavy physique with powerful thrusts and utilizing his reach to blast foes out of the *dohyo* (ring). His breakthrough moment was a 13-2 January *basho*, where he narrowly lost the division championship to his Japanese rival Takanohana.

In the spring he went 13-2 again and won promotion to the penultimate level, *ozeki*. Another great *gaijin*, Konishiki, had recently made it this far but was denied in his efforts to become *yokozuna*, mostly because of his controversial remarks and outsized personality. A Japanese novelist published an essay entitled "We Do Not Need a Foreign Yokozuna."

Diplomatically ignoring jingoistic critics and the seeming prejudice of some members of the Yokozuna Promotion Board, which decides the fate and rank of sumo champions, Akebono plowed forward. Whereas one board member said that no foreigner could possibly possess the requisite *hinkaku* (roughly, dignity and character), Akebono told the press "Never once was I treated differently."

After a broken toe knocked him out of competition for a few months, he returned with a fury, winning consecutive championships in November of 1992 and January of 1993. He could not be denied, and the watershed cultural moment occurred—Akebono was promoted to *yokozuna*.

His reign at the top of the game lasted eight years, and on the day that he was ceremoniously welcomed into the most elite rank, he honorably said, "Right now, I feel more Japanese than American."

SUMO SIZE ME At 6'8" and 500 pounds, the colossal Akebono (right) pushed his way to the rank of *yokozuna* (grand champion)—the first non-Japanese to do so in the history of the sport.

As I have said before in this book, numbers have played a major part in the history of sports. Be it records, uniform numbers of our favorite stars, or even scores of the most important games, there is meaning in numbers.

Unfortunately for some fans, there are numbers that are remembered for infamous reasons.

The Tampa Bay Bucs, a team I enjoy watching as a season-ticket holder, did not get off to a good start. For almost two full seasons, the Bucs failed to win a game. That's right, the numbers 0-26 tell the story, my friends. Finally the team broke through and over the years, there was even a world championship!

Think about the 9.79 posted by Ben Johnson of Canada in the Olympics. That statistic did not count for long since Johnson failed a drug test and was stripped of his gold, his glory, and his dignity.

Another number with a nine in it: 9-73. The Sixers under Roy Rubin and Kevin Loughery had the worst record in NBA history. That 1972-73 club won 30 games the season before. At times that club had some pretty good basketball talent—Fred Carter, Hal Greer, Bill Bridges, Tom Van Ardsdale. Ouch.

There was a famous play featuring Colorado and Missouri. In this day and age, with replays and scrutiny of clock and score, it is hard to believe that the fifth down really happened and it led to a touchdown.

The number 1919 marked the year of baseball's Black Sox scandal. Talk about giving a sport a black eye. Back then there was limited media coverage; imagine if something like that ever happened in this era?

Speaking of Chicago baseball and infamy, a name that goes hand-in-hand is Bartman. The Cubs have had an incredible drought, and just when the team was making a World Series charge, there was the foul ball heard around the world. That changed a series, and the Florida Marlins eventually moved on past the cursed Cubs. I feel bad for Mr. Bartman as he is blamed for keeping the Chitown Cubs cursed.

Dick Vitale

BUMBLIN', STUMBLIN', FUMBLIN'

*Numbers That Are Remembered for
All the Wrong Reasons*

0-26

The Bucs

Bad would be kind. So would awful, inept, and pathetic.

Let's just leave it at this: 0-26. Insert your own adjective.

In their first two seasons, the expansion Tampa Bay Buccaneers had as rude a welcoming to the NFL as one could imagine, unless, of course, you were playing them. In that case, you rolled out the green carpet and penciled in a victory.

Added to the league along with the Seattle Seahawks for the 1976 season, the Bucs debuted with an 0-14 record, making them the NFL's last winless team and the only one since 1944 failing to manage at least a tie. They followed that inauspicious entry by opening 1977 at 0-12, spiraling their losing streak to 26 games before finally tasting victory.

Going in, the team's game plan made sense (and, down the road, worked), with owner Hugh Culverhouse entrusting John McKay, USC's outstanding coach, to build his team. The Bucs spent their number-one draft pick on Okla-homa defensive end—and future Hall of Famer—Lee Roy Selmon and, to excite the local fan base, traded for former University of Florida quarterback Steve Spurrier. But without enough talent and not nearly enough depth, the situation quickly devolved.

Housed in the rugged AFC West, the Bucs were blanked, 20-0, by the Houston Oilers in their first-ever game. They were shut out again in their home opener, 23-0, by the San Diego Chargers. It took until Week 4 to score a touchdown, and that came on a fumble return.

The team's best "first chance" for a win took place on October 17 in the "Expansion Bowl" against Seattle, but the visiting Seahawks sprung to an early lead and blocked a last-minute field-goal attempt to cart away a 13-10 triumph. One week later Tampa gave Sunshine State brethren Miami a fierce battle but fell again. In Week 9, they actually had the Broncos on the ropes, leading 13-10 midway through the third quarter. Denver then scored the game's final 38 points.

And that was about it. No game the rest of the season was closer than 17 points, and for the year the Bucs were outscored 412-125. At one point McKay was asked what he thought of his team's offensive execution. The coach deadpanned, "I'm all for it."

To bolster that anemic attack, McKay used his top draft pick on running back Ricky Bell, whom he had recruited to Southern Cal. Things, instead, got worse. The Bucs were blanked six times in their first 12 games, during which they amassed 53 points...and 23 of those came in a loss at Seattle.

On December 11, 1977, the Bucs headed to New Orleans burdened with the crippling weight of a 26-game skid, during which only three games had been decided by less than a touchdown. This one wouldn't be close either, but for the first time, Tampa Bay was on the winning sideline.

They led at halftime, a rarity in itself, on a pair of Dave Green field goals and a short Gary Huff–to–Morris Owens touchdown pass that made it 13-0. On the Saints' first possession after intermission, cornerback Mike Washington grabbed an interception and raced back 45 yards for another score. With a 20-point lead, a win appeared possible. In fact, the game never got close; Tampa tacked on two more defensive touchdowns and won going away, 33-14.

Above the desire to snap the longest losing streak the league had ever seen, Buccaneer players were motivated for another reason. McKay

had read them remarks supposedly made by Saints quarterback Archie Manning that a loss to Tampa would be "disgraceful." That rallying cry, however, was news to Manning.

"I didn't know anything about it until after the game when McKay said something," Manning told *NFL Insider*'s Sal Maiorana in a 2001 interview. "None of that surfaced in New Orleans before the game because I never said it. We weren't good enough [for me] to be saying that."

Manning believes the controversy sprung out of a discussion he had with Chicago running back Walter Payton. The Bears were coming off a tough game with Tampa, and while acknowledging the Bucs had improved, Payton said it would be a disgrace to be the first to lose to them. Manning didn't disagree. Payton then mentioned the conversation to the Chicago media, which spun the story that McKay picked up on.

More than 8,000 fans greeted the team upon its triumphant return to town. By the end of the next week, they could celebrate a winning streak: the Bucs closed out the season with a 17-7 triumph over the St. Louis Cardinals.

Those wins served as a springboard of sorts. Quarterback Doug Williams was added in 1978, and a year later, when Bell rushed for a career-high 1,263 yards, the team came within one game of the Super Bowl. By then, the adjectives used to describe the Buccaneers were much kinder.

Fifth Down

Q: HOW DOES A HEROIC GOAL-LINE STAND BECOME A HEARTBREAKING FAILURE?
A: WHEN THE TEAM WITH THE BALL IS ALLOWED A *FIFTH* DOWN, AND THEY FINALLY SCORE. SORT OF.

COLORADO, 33, MISSOURI, 31

You can call it The Day That Colorado Buffaloed the Refs, call it The Mathematical Misery of Mizzou, call it what you will, but most sports fans simply call it one of the biggest blunders in history.

In 1990, the underdog Missouri Tigers were playing their hearts out on Faurot Field in front of 48,856 screaming hometown fans, and with 2:32 remaining, they'd taken a 31-27 lead against their bitter Big 8 rivals, nationally ranked Colorado. The number twelve team in the nation at the time, Coach Bill McCartney's Buffaloes sported a 3-1-1 record, with two victories and a tie against Top-20 teams, and were playing without injured star quarterback Darian Hagan. However, backup Charles Johnson was having a good game, and with All-American running back Eric Bieniemy rushing for 217 yards on the day, he marched Colorado down the treacherously slick field in the last two minutes.

A pass completion to tight end John Boman pushed the ball down to the Tigers' 3½-yard line with 31 seconds remaining. Johnson spiked the ball on first down to give the team time to strategize. Since they were trailing by four points, a field goal would do Colorado no good. They had to score a touchdown.

They then ran Bieniemy into the line. He surged forward for about two yards but was stopped a good yard from the goal line. The Buffaloes spent their last timeout with 18 seconds left on the scoreboard, which also incorrectly indicated that it was second down.

(Authors' Note: Most written accounts of this confusing game seem to indicate that the sideline markers weren't changed after the second-down play and that "two" second-down plays were run. However, broadcast footage reveals the announcers stumbling and calling Bieniemy's first rushing attempt a "first-down" play. It seems likely that some of the officials were under the impression that a timeout was called prior to Johnson spiking the ball.)

Undaunted and apparently unaware of the mix-up, the Buffs tried Bieniemy's number again, but a high-flying leap up the gut was stuffed by an inspired Mizzou defense. With the clock ticking down to just two seconds and the sideline marker incorrectly reading "3," Johnson quickly spiked the ball again. Of course, that should have been the end of the game, with Missouri taking over on downs.

Only, in some kind of Twilight Zone collective brain-freeze, fourth down had magically become third down and nobody within earshot of the officials protested. "It was kind of a bizarre deal," admitted Johnson years later.

Exacerbating matters further was the next play. On their extra fourth down, the Buffaloes ran a quarterback sneak off right tackle. Johnson was hit solidly at the 1-yard line as he cut back to the inside. His body bounced, shy of the goal line yet again, with his arms outstretched.

Jubilant Missouri fans stormed the field, howling at their hard-fought upset victory and attempting to take down the goal posts. The only problem was the officials signaled that Johnson had scored. TV replays show that it was possible though unlikely that he did, but that decision was final.

Then it gradually dawned on people that the tainted touchdown call was not even close to being the biggest mistake the referees had made. The tape definitely showed that Colorado had run five consecutive offensive plays after they had first-and-goal at the 3. That don't add up.

"Fans were charging the refs, Missouri players were charging the refs," Tigers quarterback Kent Kiefer recalled ten years later. "There were objects being thrown at them. It was complete chaos."

Referee J.C. Louderback was on the phone with league officials for several agonizing minutes before he gave the bad news to the boisterous crowd. The touchdown stood. After taking a knee on the extra point attempt, Colorado had "won" the game, 33-31.

"People always ask me if I was involved in the 'Fifth Down Game' against Missouri, and my comment is always, 'Yep, I called all five plays,'" joked Gerry DiNardo, Colorado's offensive coordinator at the time. "I'm just glad I didn't need a sixth."

The Big 8 suspended all seven officials who worked the game, but the decision was not overturned, with Commissioner Carl James ruling that it was "not a correctable error." Louderback never commented publicly about the game, apparently taking the...Fifth.

And if there was any solace to be had for Missouri, which finished the season 4–7, it was that they, by all reasonable accounts, defeated the national champions that year. After capping off the season with a stirring 10–9 Fiesta Bowl victory over Notre Dame, Colorado finished with a record of 10–1–1. Georgia Tech, with a record of 11–0–1, won the honors in the coaches' poll, but Colorado was voted a share of the national championship in the sportswriters' poll, which just goes to show you that writers aren't so good at math.

7

VAN DE VELDE'S MELTDOWN AT THE BRITISH OPEN
TOOK HIM FROM FAME TO SHAME.

Jean Van de Velde

Clang, glug, glug. So long, Claret Jug.

Jean Van de Velde was just one hole away from wrapping up his first major at the British Open in 1999, needing only a double-bogey 6 on the par-4 18th hole at Carnoustie Golf Links in Scotland to enter the winner's circle and take hold of the ancient trophy.

Sadist spoiler alert—instead, the fearless Frenchman carded a seven. As in Dante's seven levels of purgatory.

Knowing that he needed just a 6 to secure victory, Van de Velde hit a driver into light winds off the tee at 18. He wound up veering wide right and landed in the rough just off the adjoining 17th fairway. Not pretty, but quite playable, and the native of Biarritz had spent the whole tournament scrambling out of trouble. His 5-shot cushion to start the day had evaporated with five bogeys on the first 12 holes, but then he righted the ship enough on the back nine to have the tournament in hand.

Almost everybody in attendance expected Van de Velde to lay up short of a water-filled trench

called the Barry Burn, leaving himself an easy chip to the green, where a 3-putt would still clinch victory and the first British Open title for a Frenchman in 92 years. After all, Carnoustie is perhaps the toughest links course in all of Britain, billing itself as a "daunting cocktail of gales, thick rough, and devilish bunkers."

But Van de Velde had other ideas. He'd birdied the daunting 18 on Friday and Saturday and saw a clear line over the water, where he could go out in style with a par. As he recalled stage one of his very public meltdown:

"I only had 185 [yards] to carry the water, which wasn't very demanding," he said. "The only thing you didn't have to do was hit it left. So do you hit a wedge down the left side and then pitch on the green, or do you hit a shot over there and try to move forward with it?

"The ball was lying so good, I took my 2-iron.... I pushed it a little. I didn't hit a very good shot."

He pushed it a lot. The ball ricocheted off the grandstands and bounced off the rocks

FRENCH DIP Jean Van de Velde had the British Open championship in his back pocket until his risky decision-making on the final hole led to a nightmarish triple bogey.

surrounding Barry Burn, landing short of the hazard and in the "daunting cocktail" that was now beginning to look like hemlock. Lying two, with no obvious play except a lateral punch-out, the aggressive Van de Velde was about to enter the next level of his nightmare.

"I couldn't go backwards, I don't think I could have done anything," he said. "The only thing I could do was try to hit it hard. Obviously I didn't hit it hard enough or get it out as I wanted."

Indeed, his third shot from the deep rough faltered and ended up in the creek. Now the planned victory parade down 18 was turning into a surreal, detour-laden funeral march. Stoically and somewhat absurdly, this golfer who had never before been in contention for a major removed his shoes, thinking that he might be able to play the ball out of the water.

His ball was visible but submerged. Playing partner Craig Parry of Australia, already out of contention himself, walked over and dropped a little gallows humor: "Just wait a little longer; the tide's going out."

Wisely, Van de Velde re-shod and took a penalty drop. He was now lying four. At this point the crowd was standing stunned in the light grey drizzle. Their daylong chants of "Allez Jean" in thick British accents, having been won over by this stylish foreign qualifier, had now dissipated into murmurs and gasps.

Justin Leonard and Paul Lawrie were already in the clubhouse with scores of +6, assuming they'd be splitting the second-place money. But news of the recent sequence had them sitting up and taking notice.

Despite the horrifying turn of events, the tournament was still there for the Frenchman's taking. Van de Velde needed to "get up and down"—put the ball on the green with this shot and sink his putt to save double-bogey 6. Rattled as he was, though, he got under the ball and knocked it into the sand trap.

The closest eyewitness to this tragicomedy, somewhat reminiscent of the Kevin Costner movie *Tin Cup*, was Parry. "I was really feeling for Jean on 18," he said. "I could see him throwing the tournament away. He played great for 71 holes. I feel sorry for him."

Then, just when it seemed that he had gambled himself right out of the British Open, Van de Velde regrouped and stopped the bleeding. He coolly knocked his bunker shot on the green, about five or six feet away. In dead silence, Van de Velde calmly sank his triple-bogey putt to salvage a spot in a playoff with Lawrie and Leonard.

Eerily, Van de Velde had foreshadowed just such a turn of events when he addressed the press after he took the lead in the second round. "I've always been playing well, it just hasn't quite gone my way," he said. "Maybe I've faded because of bad strategy or something, but I'm very happy it happened here."

Lawrie won the four-hole playoff handily, and Van de Velde handled his meltdown with aplomb, even appearing to be somewhat amused by the hand-wringing reaction of the media and fans.

"Maybe it was asking too much for me," the Frenchman shrugged. "Maybe I should have laid up. The ball was laying so well.... Next time, I hit a wedge, and you all forgive me?"

65—whoops, 66 at Roberto De Vicenzo's Masters of Disaster

It was the worst birthday present ever. Argentinean golf pro Roberto De Vicenzo turned 45 years old on the final day of the Masters tournament on April 14, 1968. He shot an impressive 65 on the day—but he carded a 66—and missed out on a playoff with Bob Goalby, who was declared the outright victor even though they each took 277 shots (-11) to complete the four days of golf.

It seems that playing partner Tommy Aaron incorrectly wrote down a 4 instead of a 3 for De Vicenzo after the 17th hole. De Vicenzo signed and turned in the card without catching the mistake, and that was all she wrote.

"Under the rules of golf," Hord Hardin, president of the U.S. Golf Association and chairman of the rules committee, said in a statement, "he [De Vicenzo] will be charged with a 66, which does not leave him in a tie with Bob Goalby, who is 11 under par. He is second, 10 under par."

A wretched way to end the day for the talented Argentinean, who had begun it by holing out a 130-yard, 9-iron shot for eagle on the first hole. Aaron was visibly upset at his clerical error, staying around only long enough to say, "I realized I had made an error before I left the official table. I looked around for Roberto, but he was gone. There was a general state of confusion. I wish I could have done something but the damage was done."

Although the incident inspired De Vicenzo to utter the immortal golf quote, "What a stupid I am," he could take consolation in a fantastic career that landed him in the World Golf Hall of Fame, with over 200 international titles to his credit, including nine Argentinean Opens, one British Open (1967), and the 1980 U.S. Senior Open.

ROW 8, AISLE 4, SEAT 113

The Chicago Cubs

At least the long-suffering Red Sox Nation had the romance of the "Curse of the Bambino." Cubs fans are stuck with the saga of the Foul Ball Fiasco.

Wrigley Field was rocking on the night of October 14, 2003. Their beloved Cubbies hadn't been to the World Series in 58 years, but they were just five outs away. It was Game 6 of the National League Championship Series, and ace Mark Prior was shutting down the Florida Marlins, 3-0, with one out in the top of the eighth inning.

Speedy Juan Pierre had a decent lead off second, but Prior pounded one in on Luis Castillo, and the Marlins second baseman slung a lazy pop-up down the left-field line, right where the stands jut toward the field in the cozy little bandbox of a park. Left fielder Moises Alou, a solid defensive player, had a clear bead on the ball, gauged where the brick wall was, and leapt up, glove outstretched, to bring down the second out of the inning.

But instead, a young Cubs fan named Steve Bartman, who was sitting adjacent to the field in Row 8, Aisle 4, Seat 113, simply tried to catch the souvenir that was heading right for him. In the process, he unwittingly prevented Alou from making the play and entered the annals of doom.

The outfielder was clearly disgusted. The Cubs were soon deflated.

Because the ball was not in the field of play, it could not be ruled as fan interference. Castillo wound up drawing a walk. Miguel Cabrera hit a grounder that looked like a double-play ball, but shortstop Alex Gonzalez made an error, and all runners were safe. Eight runs later, the nightmarish inning was over. Bartman had to be escorted out of Wrigley Field by security, as the Cubs wound up losing the game.

The next day Bartman's brother-in-law read his statement to the press: "I am so truly sorry from the bottom of this Cubs fan's broken heart," it said.

"I ask that Cub fans everywhere redirect the negative energy that has been vented towards my family, my friends, and myself into the usual positive support for our beloved team on their way to being National League champs," Bartman added.

Instead, the team lost Game 7 and the NLCS to the Marlins, who went on to capture the World Series over the Yankees. Four years later, and the tough-luck Cubbies were still flat on their backs, 62 years removed from their last pennant. However, that seat still stands, taunting the team and its fans. "They blew up the [infamous] ball," Cubs fan Brad Rendell told the Knight-Ridder news service a year later. "I think they should rip the seat out and blow it up, too. They'd get a huge crowd."

It's not all his fault.

Entering baseball's 2007 season, the Cubs owned the longest drought between World Series championships, last winning the title in 1908. And you can't blame it all on Steve Bartman. They're believed to be under the spell of the "Billy Goat Curse," cast upon them by William Sianis, who was kicked out of Wrigley Field for bringing his pet goat to Game 4 of the 1945 World Series. While being ushered from the park, Sianis condemned the Cubs to never win a championship, yelling, "The Cubs ain't gonna win no more. The Cubs will never win a World Series so long as the goat is not allowed in Wrigley Field."

9-73

SUFFERING THROUGH A LOST SEASON IN THE CITY OF BROTHERLY LOVE.

Philadelphia 76ers

Champagne is the toast of choice for the 1972 Miami Dolphins players upon learning their status as the only perfect team in NFL history is safe for another season.

So how do you think members of the 1972-73 Philadelphia 76ers respond when they realize their record will stay intact for another year? By doubling their medication?

Those 76ers, you see, are the undisputed worst team in the history of professional basketball. And there are 73 reasons why. Make that nine wins and 73 losses why.

That disastrous campaign marked the final thud for a franchise that just six years earlier ruled the NBA with arguably the greatest team ever assembled. Philadelphia's 1966-67 lineup featured superstars Wilt Chamberlain and Hal Greer, along with Chet Walker, Luke Jackson, Wally Jones, Billy Cunningham, Larry Costello, and Matt Guokas. They won 45 of their first 49 games and finished 68-13, knocked out the Celtics in the Eastern Conference Finals (depriv-

ing Boston a shot at a ninth straight title), and then beat the San Francisco Warriors in six games to take the championship.

The descent was gradual: Philly won 62 games the following year but was beaten by the Celtics in the playoffs. Then, before the start of the 1968-69 campaign, general manager/head coach Jack Ramsay shipped Chamberlain to the Lakers. The victory total dipped to 55. By 1971-72 they had fallen to 30-52. Cunningham, by now an All-Star, bolted for the dollars available in the rival American Basketball Association. Other players got old. Trades were bad. And the draft yielded little—the team's first-round draft picks included Craig Raymond, Shaler Halimon, Bud Ogden, Al Henry, Dana Lewis, and Fred Boyd. Don't look for any of their plaques at the Basketball Hall of Fame. Even Ramsay skipped town, taking on a similar role with the Buffalo Braves.

In a desperate search for a "name" coach who could minimize the impending disaster and jumpstart a rebuilding effort, the 76ers approached Marquette guru Al McGuire and then-70-year-old Adolph Rupp, winner of four NCAA titles at the University of Kentucky. The answers were "no" and "no." So they rolled the dice with an eager collegiate coach named Roy Rubin, who in 11 seasons at Long Island University amassed a nifty .649 winning percentage.

Rubin shined with optimism, despite knowing the challenge he faced. "I'm giving up a lot," he said the day he was hired. "Another guy might say, 'Gee...he's got to be out of his skull.'"

More appropriate might be to wonder what was inside his skull. The year started with a 95-89 loss at Chicago. Then there was a 105-100 setback to Seattle in the team's home opener. That was followed by a three-point home loss to Ramsay's Braves and a defeat four nights later in Buffalo. But 0-4 sounds pretty good compared to 0-15, which the 76ers were before they finally won a game, a 114-112 tussle over the Houston Rockets. Even that win came with a price—Rubin pulled a leg muscle during the game.

They then dropped six more before getting revenge on Ramsay with a 101-94 victory in Buffalo. They won their first home game in their 12th attempt, beating the Kansas City-Omaha Kings by five points. After nosediving to 4-47 following an 11-point loss to the Baltimore Bullets, Rubin was mercifully dismissed. (Having had his fill of basketball, he went on to own an International House of Pancakes restaurant in Miami.) Veteran guard Kevin Loughery took over as player/coach and actually managed to coax a pair of two-game winning streaks out of the beleaguered team that raised their record to

9-60. But just when the team appeared to be jelling, they ended the season with 13 straight losses. At least Philly fans were wise enough to avert their eyes; the 76ers drew fewer than 6,000 fans per game to the Spectrum.

For the record, the team was not completely devoid of talent. Guard Fred Carter averaged a team-high 20.0 points per game and Tom Van Arsdale scored at a 17.7 points-per-game clip. Leroy Ellis, a solid inside player, contributed 13.7 points per game and 10.8 rebounds per game. But they didn't have much help.

BILLY CUNNINGHAM, No. 32, shoots against the Los Angeles Lakers. (photo courtesy Getty Images)

AT THE 1988 OLYMPICS, BIG BEN CLOCKED THE FASTEST 100M TIME EVER. BUT HE DIDN'T BRING HOME THE GOLD.

9.79

Ben Johnson

For 14 years, Ben Johnson was technically the fastest man on the planet. On the biggest stage there was, the 1988 Seoul Olympics, the muscular Canadian sprinter exploded out of the blocks and blazed past his bitter rival, Carl Lewis of the United States, for a world-record time of 9.79 seconds in the 100-meter race. He even eased off the gas a little at the end as he broke the tape to raise his arm in victory and glance over at Lewis.

"If I had gone through I would have got 9.75," said Johnson. "But I'm saving that for next year."

However, with the biggest stage comes the biggest spotlight, with the biggest scrutiny. Three days later the results from a post-race drug test found that Johnson's urine contained stanozolol, a performance-enhancing steroid so strong it is known to cause kidney cancer.

For that, Johnson had to forfeit the race and the gold medal. Lewis was awarded the gold, and his time of 9.92 was anointed as the new world record. That's because Johnson's magnif-

icent 9.83 at the 1987 World Championships in Rome was also stricken from the record books, while his country was just plain stricken. "A national tragedy," declared Canadian Prime Minister Brian Mulroney.

Making matters worse, Johnson compounded the shame by admitting that yes, he had taken performance-enhancing drugs in the past, but claiming, without evidence, that somebody had spiked his drink right after the race.

In Seoul, after the news was announced, many track athletes were pleased that their sport was being policed. "I'm happy they caught a big fish," said Brazilian 800-meter silver-medalist Joachim Cruz. "I'm thinking of the hundreds of athletes who train naturally all year. This is good for the sport."

Johnson was definitely just the tip of the iceberg, as disqualifications and suspensions have littered the sport for the past two decades. Some cynics have called that final in Seoul "The Dirtiest Race in History," as four of the top five finishers, including silver-medalist Linford Christie and American Dennis Mitchell, were all subsequently implicated in doping cases.

Lewis, who had frequently intimated that Johnson was on steroids, said only, "I feel sorry for Ben and the Canadian people."

For his actions, the recalcitrant Johnson was suspended from the sport for two years and made a less-than-successful comeback, reaching only the semifinals of the 1992 Barcelona Olympics. Then he tested positive again in 1993 and was suspended once more. And just to make sure he didn't soil his chemically enhanced reputation, Johnson was suspended again in 1999, even though by then he was far past his prime.

His time of 9.79, although nullified, went unsurpassed until American Tim Montgomery posted a 9.78 in 2002. But that time has been officially discredited as well, continuing the sport's recent steroid sorrows. After testifying that he obtained steroids and human growth hormone from BALCO, Montgomery was stripped of all his post-2001 records. Fortunately, the new record of 9.77, set by Jamaica's Asafa Powell, is both amazing and legitimate.

Johnson's bitterness has not gone away with the years. In a 2006 interview with Australian TV, he was still adamant, 18 years after the fact, that he'd been railroaded.

"Number one, that day the drugs that they find in my system was not the drugs that I was using," he said.

"Number two, Ben Johnson was sabotaged in Seoul. Somebody set me up."

Johnson has set up a strange life for himself since the shame of Seoul, even at one point training Libyan dictator Muammar al-Qaddafi's son in soccer. Most recently he made dubious headlines by appearing in commercials for a Canadian energy drink called Cheetah Power Surge. The owner of the company asks him, "Ben, when you run, do you Cheetah?" And Ben says: "Absolutely. I Cheetah all the time."

ROID TO RUIN Canadian sprinter Ben Johnson was called the "fastest man on the planet" until a failed drug test took away his 1988 Olympic gold medal.

W50

FOR ROSIE RUIZ, IT WAS ONE IF BY LAND, TWO IF BY SEA, AND THREE IF BY MASS TRANSIT.

Rosie Ruiz

Winning the Boston Marathon requires skill, stamina, and speed.

Or, failing all that, a public transit token and chutzpah like you wouldn't believe.

On April 21, 1980, a Cuban-American woman from New York named Rosie Ruiz was crowned the winner of the Boston Marathon in the female division with a record time of 2:31:56. After crossing the finish line, 26.2 miles from the start, and six miles beyond Heartbreak Hill, Rosie grimaced like someone who'd been through a lot. And maybe she had, but it sure wasn't running.

Nobody could remember seeing her or her number "W50" on Heartbreak Hill, or along most of the course, for that matter. Shortly after the finish, some witnesses placed her emerging from a "T" station (Boston's public transit system) less than a mile from the finish, and the controversy was on. Of course, these days there are on-course video cameras, separate starts for the elite runners, and more stringent checkpoints to ensure that such things don't happen, but guess whose stunt helped create the need for such measures?

Ruiz accepted the award and the adulation that day and adamantly denied the allegations, even though she couldn't describe many of the landmarks on the route, and was completely unfamiliar with running terms such as "intervals" and "splits." Although there was no hard photographic evidence either way, race officials eventually decided to strip Ruiz of her title and named Jacqueline Gareau of Montreal as the women's winner, with a time of 2:34:28.

Bolstering the case against Rosie's Ruse, as it became known, was the fact that months later, New York Marathon director Fred Lebow nullified Ruiz's official 1979 finish (which qualified her for Boston), after eyewitness accounts proved conclusively that Ruiz had hopped the subway and shortcut that marathon, too.

Ruiz never officially finished a marathon, and two years later was arrested for larceny and forgery. In 1984 she was arrested for conspiring to sell two kilos of cocaine to undercover agents, but is out of prison now, living a quiet life in Florida.

NO SWEAT Rosie Ruiz "won" the women's division of the Boston Marathon in 1980, but she was stripped of the title when it was determined that she took mass transit and ran only a small portion of the 26.2-mile course.

RED SOX FANS DIDN'T HAVE TO WAIT AN ETERNITY BETWEEN WORLD SERIES TITLES. IT JUST SEEMED THAT WAY.

86

The Red Sox

NUMBELIEVABLE

"Twenty-Ninety. Twenty-Ninety."

Those Yankee fans can be so cute, can't they, for that was their chant following the Red Sox's long-awaited triumph in the 2004 World Series. They figured their Beantown rivals should be ready for another championship in 86 more years.

The funny thing is that up until 1918, the Red Sox were a dynasty—take that, Bronx Bombers—winning five crowns in the fall classic's first 15 years. The final title drew an underwhelming response from spoiled Sox supporters; a meager 15,238 bothered to attend the 2-1 series-clincher over the Cubs at Fenway Park.

"[Their attitude] was, 'It's another championship for our boys. That's great. They'll be back again,'" said Richard Johnson, longtime curator of the New England Sports Museum. "Little did they know it would be 86 years."

Of course they'd keep winning. Those regal Red Sox employed Babe Ruth, the game's rising star whose swing and swagger would popular-ize the sport over the next two decades. In his early career, Ruth was also a lethal lefty on the mound and had won a pair of games in the 1918 Series. But on January 5, 1920, cash-strapped owner Harry Frazee sold Ruth to the New York Yankees for $100,000 (and a $300,000 loan) so he could pay off old debts and the mortgage on Fenway Park.

It's rumored that Frazee then walked beneath a ladder, opened an umbrella inside his house, and shattered a mirror. (The most devout in Red Sox Nation contend he also drank pig's blood.) For on that fateful day, the "Curse of the Bam-bino" was born. From 1919 through 2003, while the Yankees were racking up 26 World Championships, the Sox won zero. As in none. And to magnify the torture, four times Boston found itself on the precipice of a title only to drop Game 7 in each Series.

The first frustration came in 1946 when St. Louis's Enos Slaughter broke a late-inning tie by hustling all the way from first on Harry Walker's bloop double, catching the Sox (most notably shortstop Johnny Pesky, who momentarily hesitated before making his relay throw home) by surprise. In 1967 the Red Sox were too swept up in the "Impossible Dream" to lament the reality of another series loss to the Cardinals. They gamely battled a superior St. Louis team but were no match for Bob Gibson (whom *Boston* *Globe* scribe Jim McCabe described as "think Pedro Martinez and Roger Clemens, put 'em together, and you have Gibson"), who pitched three complete-game wins, including a 7-2 laugher in the finale.

The 1975 World Series against the Reds also reached a seventh game after the Game 6 heroics of Bernie Carbo, who tied things up with a

JOHNNY ON THE SPOT Johnny Damon accepts the congratulations of teammates during the Red Sox's 2004 World Series triumph, Boston's first in 86 seasons.

three-run pinch-hit homer in the eighth inning, and Carlton Fisk, whose dramatic foul-pole clanger in the twelfth earned the Sox a 7-6 victory. But in the final game, with the score knotted in the ninth inning, the Reds' Joe Morgan lofted a broken-bat two-out single into center that plated Ken Griffey with the winning run.

Boston's next dose of World Series agony came in 1986. Yes, the Sox were one strike away...on three different occasions. But the Mets rallied with three runs in the bottom of the tenth inning to steal Game 6, the tiebreaker crossing the plate when Mookie Wilson's soft bouncer evaded the glove of Sox first baseman Bill Buckner. New York then trailed, 3-0, in Game 7 but again rallied to hand the Red Sox one of the most devastating defeats in World Series lore.

However, in 2004, just when it seemed certain the title-less streak would reach 86 years, the Red Sox staged the greatest comeback in baseball history. Funny how that happens, isn't it? After dropping the first three games of the American League Championship Series to the Yankees—including a 19-8 embarrassment in Game 3—Boston's only option appeared to be choosing its form of execution.

But as sportswriter/author Dan Shaughnessy observed prior to Game 4: "They [the Sox] were surprisingly composed and confident while perched on the brink of extinction. They truly believed they could dig out of this hole, and there was odd comfort in the knowledge that no one outside the clubhouse thought they could do it."

The Sox got thrown a lifeline in Game 4, tying it up in their final at-bat and winning, 6-4, on David Ortiz's twelfth-inning blast. Game 5 had the same score and same hero; this time Ortiz laced an RBI single in the bottom of the fourteenth as the Sox won 5-4. Curt Schilling and his bloody sock were the story of Game 6. And in Game 7 Boston became the executioner, hanging the Yankees with a 10-3 loss in front of a disbelieving Yankee Stadium crowd.

In the World Series the Red Sox swept the Cardinals—their antagonists in 1946 and 1967—in four straight. "The final game, a 3-0 Sox win, was more coronation than contest," wrote Shaughnessy in his book *Reversing the Curse*. "It was the night of simultaneous celestial events—a total lunar eclipse and the Red Sox winning a World Series."

Three days later more than 3 million Red Sox fans poured into the city for a victory parade they waited 86 years to attend. No one was taking this title stuff for granted any more.

1919

The Black Sox BASEBALL'S GREATEST SCANDAL LEFT A BLACK MARK ON THE GAME.

The tabloid name for baseball's dirtiest laundry was actually inspired by...dirty laundry. What you might find even more surprising is that the infamous Chicago White Sox of 1919 were actually christened the "Black Sox" by themselves the year before their World Series gambling scandal.

As the legend goes, Sox owner Charles A. Comiskey, a former first baseman, was notoriously tight-fisted. In 1918 his penury extended even into the locker room, where he refused to pay for his team's uniforms to be washed. In protest, his players took the field in progressively filthier flannels for several weeks, calling themselves the Black Sox to spite their cheap employer.

But no amount of detergent would be able to wash away the stain that was put on the game in 1919. As painstakingly chronicled in Eliot Asinof's groundbreaking book *Eight Men Out* and numerous follow-ups, many of those same slighted White Sox came under question for taking money from gamblers and "throwing" the

World Series to the Cincinnati Reds, who won the best-of-nine series, five games to three. Some of the White Sox publicly admitted their transgressions, while others went to their graves denying that they'd done anything wrong.

In the end, eight White Sox players and a number of known gamblers were indicted in 1920 on "conspiracy to defraud the public and injure the business of Charles A. Comiskey and the American League." Although they were acquitted in 1921 by a Cook County grand jury under some fairly suspicious circumstances ("lost" testimony from two of the players), on the very next day, all eight players would be barred from organized baseball for life.

The circumstances leading up to the tawdry episode were as follows:

The Reds were a decent club, with 96 wins under their belt, but they had six regulars who batted .276 or lower. The powerful White Sox had only two below that level. On top of that, they came from the superior American League (winners of the last four World Series, including the White Sox themselves in 1917) and they had two of the most sparkling pitchers of the day, control master Eddie Cicotte (29-7; 1.82 ERA) and Lefty Williams (23-11; 2.64 ERA). It was generally assumed that these brilliant White Sox would manhandle the Reds in the World Series.

"They were the best," said Chicago second baseman Eddie Collins, who'd already played for Connie Mack's championship Philadelphia Athletics clubs, and was not included in the indictments. "There never was a ball club like that."

However, the team was a very fractious bunch, driven to distraction by their low salaries and conflicting personalities. Nearly everyone resented the college-educated Collins, who also made more money than anybody else. According to Geoffrey C. Ward and Ken Burns's *Baseball: An Illustrated History*, they even froze him out of pregame practice sessions, and first baseman Chick Gandil didn't speak to him for two years.

It was Gandil, a 31-year-old tough guy who'd been a hobo and a boilermaker, who was the ringleader of the dubious scandal. Through a

DIRTY SOX Eight members of the Chicago White Sox were banned from baseball for life after it was determined they conspired to "throw" the 1919 World Series.

small-time gambler friend, Joseph "Sport" Sullivan, Gandil let it be known that for the price of $100,000, the heavily favored White Sox would "throw" the World Series to the Reds. Big-time New York gambler Arnold "Mr. Bankroll" Rothstein was purportedly behind those financing the deal.

Gandil allegedly lined up seven other players to get in on the deal, including the two pitching aces, Cicotte and Williams. Sportswriter Hugh Fullerton had heard all the rumors and noticed that his hotel's lobby was crawling with known gamblers. Before a pitch was even thrown, he wired all the papers that carried his column: "Advise All Not to Bet on This Series. Ugly Rumors Afloat."

Fullerton's suspicions seemed confirmed on the second pitch of Game 1, when the razor-sharp Cicotte, who'd led the American League in wins and the lowest walks-per-inning ratio, plunked Reds leadoff batter Morrie Rath right between the shoulder blades. Many took that as a signal to the gamblers that Cicotte was on board.

The Reds beat the masterful Cicotte and roared out to a surprising lead in the Series. White Sox manager Kid Gleason was beside himself: "They aren't hitting. I don't know what the matter is, but I do know that something is wrong with my gang. The bunch I had fighting in August for the pennant would have trimmed the Cincinnati bunch without a struggle. The bunch I have now couldn't beat a high school team."

The reeling White Sox rallied to take three games, including one behind Cicotte, but that was only because some of the promised payoffs for the players were late or never arrived. Finally, the gruesome charade ended in Game 8, after Williams was allegedly issued a death threat by the antsy syndicate that feared the Sox were playing on the level and screwing up their wagers. Williams lost all three of his starts in the Series, retiring just one batter in the finale before being driven from the mound.

Although the players were acquitted in 1921, baseball owners moved quickly to save their reputation with a growling public. Newly installed commissioner Kenesaw Mountain Landis, a former federal judge, drew a very hard line and banned all eight named players for life, even those like third baseman Buck Weaver, who knew of the "fix" but never took a dime and by all accounts played his heart out.

Most famously, of course, there was the legendary "Shoeless" Joe Jackson, an illiterate country boy from South Carolina with the thunderous stroke that Babe Ruth sought to copy. Jackson admitted that he took $5,000, but claimed that he played to win as well. His .375 average in the Series bears that out, although some accounts of his fielding do not.

Although it's much debated whether the anecdote of a young guttersnipe accosting his hero on the courthouse steps and beseeching him, "Say it ain't so, Joe," is apocryphal or not, one statement that is definitely on the public record comes from the foreman of the jury in 1920: "Baseball is more than a national game. It is an American institution, [our great teacher of] respect for proper authority, self-confidence, fair-mindedness, quick judgment, and self-control."

What a way to close out this book! The crème de la crème, numbers simply awesome because of their meaning.

Start with the number seven to signify Tour de France wins by the master, Mr. Lance Armstrong. He was the pride and joy of American cycling and a true marvel. He also dominated the ESPYs for years as Best Male Athlete. My friends, I can't imagine the pain endured in the long bike run through the mountains. Talk about pressure, every year there were great expectations, and Armstrong met them.

The number 11 told us about the greatest basketball franchise in NBA history, the Boston Celtics. That number stands for the championship banners Bill Russell brought the rafters in Beantown. It also shows what Red Auerbach accomplished and how Russell, Bob Cousy, Bill Sharman, Sam Jones, K.C. Jones, and a cast of others meshed into greatness. Later on there were stars like John Havlicek. They were fun to watch.

When you talk about dominance, are you kidding me? Red Auerbach was so special, showing the ability to get the most out of his people, doing it in a brilliant fashion. They came to play—run, press, and shoot. Growing up as a coach, you had to idolize them. Watching them perform was special.

I loved seeing Auerbach light up that victory cigar. When I think of the NBA, I think of one Arnold "Red" Auerbach.

Seven hundred and fourteen and 755 are famous numbers because of our affection for the home-run record. Babe Ruth and Henry Aaron set marks that meant more than just a record for baseball fans to love. Casual sports fans know who these two gentlemen are because of those stats.

Five hundred and eleven is a number nobody will ever come close to. Cy Young won 511 baseball games, which helps explain why baseball's best pitcher is honored each season with an award with Young's name on it. These days, few pitchers challenge to get to 300 wins. Forget about 511. Do you think anyone is going to get 20 wins a season times 25 years, and even that is a drop short? Very few win 20 in one season, let alone 25 times!

Five thousand seven hundred and fourteen stands for the numbers of strikeouts thrown by Hall of Famer Nolan Ryan. It is hard to believe that anyone will challenge that mark for many years, if ever. You don't see big-time strikeout artists last long these days as injuries can take their toll.

Two hundred and eight stands out because that is the number of times legendary and classy receiver Jerry Rice reached the end zone. It will take longevity and brilliance to make a run at that mark.

Eighteen stands for the number of major golf tournaments won by the Golden Bear, Jack Nicklaus. Mr. Woods, are you listening? Tiger is off to a good start to catch and shatter that record. For now, it stands tall.

There are other special numbers in this chapter, a perfect way to conclude this exciting and intriguing journey through statistics that have made a difference in the world of sports.

Dick Vitale

PUNCH THE CLOCK

Longevity + Brilliance = All-Time Dominating Digits

AMERICANS FINALLY HAD A REASON
TO FOLLOW THE TOUR DE FRANCE

Lance Armstrong

For seven straight years the most grueling race in the world, the over-2,000-mile Tour de France, ended with Lance Armstrong ahead of the pack, donning the *maillot jaune*, the yellow winner's jersey.

On Sunday, July 24, 2005, the famed cancer survivor Armstrong rode into the sunset in stirring Hollywood style, going out on the very top of his sport, surrounded by his young twin daughters wearing yellow dresses and then-girlfriend, rock star Sheryl Crow, in a yellow halter top, while the strains of "The Star Spangled Banner" reverberated around the Champs-Élysées.

"What he did was sensational," said third-place finisher Jan Ullrich, the 1997 Tour winner and one of Armstrong's toughest competitors.

From the podium in Paris, an emotional and fiery Armstrong bid farewell to the obscure sport (in America, at least) that made him a household name: "The last thing I'll say to the people who don't believe in cycling, the cynics, and the skeptics, I'm sorry for you. I'm sorry that you can't

dream big. I'm sorry you don't believe in miracles. But this is one hell of a race. This is a great sporting event, and you should stand around and believe it. You should believe in these athletes, and you should believe in these people. I'll be a fan of the Tour de France for as long as I live. And there are no secrets—this is a hard sporting event and hard work wins it. So Vive le Tour. Forever!"

If he was a bit defensive, that's because a cloud of suspicion had begun to arise around Armstrong and his record-breaking feats. His seven titles, two more than the runners-up in that category—Frenchmen Jacques Anquetil and Bernard Hinault, Belgian Eddy Merckx, and Spaniard Miguel Indurain—came under question with ongoing allegations of illegal blood-doping. The French sporting magazine *L'Equipe* reported in October of 2005 that, thanks to advanced technological techniques, modern-day urine-testing revealed that Armstrong had been on the blood-boosting drug EPO during the

1999 Tour de France. Armstrong steadfastly denies ever having used performance-enhancing drugs.

Regardless of its ultimate veracity, the controversy does not erase the memory of one of the most stunning and uplifting comebacks in the history of sports. In October of 1996 Armstrong, then a little-known former professional triathlete and World Cycling Champion of 1993, was diagnosed with stage-three testicular cancer. Doctors found that it had metastasized to his brain, lungs, and abdomen, and his chances of survival were pegged at less than 50 percent.

Three years later, after undergoing extensive chemotherapy, he emerged from arduous training with coach Chris Carmichael and the U.S. Postal team to not only win the Tour, but to blow away the field by 7:37, one of the largest margins in the modern history of the monumental three-week, 20-stage race.

As the years rolled by and the titles piled up, Armstrong's momentum took on a life of its own. This 5'10", 170-pound winning machine was a sure bet to annihilate his competitors on the extreme uphill stages, earning him the title King of the Mountains. With his superb conditioning (a resting heart rate of 32 beats per minute) and charismatic presence, he simply dominated the field at the Hautacam stage in 2000.

Then, in 2001, he blew by archrival Ullrich on the debilitating Alpe d'Huez, with its oxygen-unfriendly 21 switchbacks, and famously looked back to gauge whether his foe had enough in the tank to keep pace. He did not. Armstrong was the beneficiary of brilliant team riding in 2002, as U.S. Postal director Johan Bruyneel's multi-

national cabal paced its leader perfectly. Armstrong deftly avoided a dangerous collision in 2003, and with the pressure on in 2004 to become the all-time winningest Tour rider, he rode heroically.

He finished his epoch with not only those seven straight championships, but 21 stage victories and 83 yellow jerseys.

LANCE ARMSTRONG holds the winner's trophy after his seventh straight Tour de France win.

THE DEFENSIVE-MINDED CENTER WON AN UNPRECEDENTED NUMBER OF CHAMPIONSHIPS— PROBABLY BECAUSE THAT'S ALL HE CARED ABOUT

Bill Russell

Bill Russell played defense like he had more than two hands, so it's only fitting that he wound up with more rings than two hands can accommodate. The legendary Boston Celtics center played 13 seasons in his career and won 11 NBA titles in that span, tying Montreal Canadiens great Maurice Richard's record for most team championships won by an individual. Although many Celtic greats played in that era, Russell was the only one active for all 11 of those championships, and the way Red Auerbach saw it, that's no coincidence.

"This is a guy who made shot-blocking an art," the late Hall of Fame coach and team president told the *Boston Globe* in the 1990s. "Today, there are very few people who know how to block shots like he did. They like to smack it away into the stands. Russ kept the ball in play and I'd say 75 percent of the time, we came up with the ball."

Russell's rookie season began late, because he went to Melbourne, Australia, and won his third championship in 18 months, starring for the U.S. Olympic basketball team that brought home the gold in 1956. "We were already in first place when he got here, but he was ready," Auerbach said. Blending the ball-hawking Russell with a coterie of savvy, sharp-shooting veterans, the Celtics became a perpetual motion machine.

The Celtics and Hawks squared off in the NBA Finals at the end of that season, with Boston and their new main cog prevailing. The Hawks returned the favor the next season, beating the Celtics, in part because Russell had the flu. For the next eight years, it was lights out for the rest of the league, kicking off the streak with a cold-blooded sweep of the Minneapolis Lakers.

Although the great Bob Cousy retired six titles into the reign, a new complement of starters and teammates, including K.C. Jones, Sam Jones, and John Havlicek, blended beautifully with the dominating No. 6. The supporting cast had changed, but the script remained the same.

Rebound. Score. Defend. Block shot. Hoist banner to rafters of Boston Garden. Repeat.

Russell was a 12-time All-Star and five-time MVP, but all he truly cared about were the championships.

The last two had even more historical significance than the first nine, because they were achieved after Auerbach retired from coaching. His successor was none other than Russell, who in 1966 became the first African American head coach in the history of American pro sports. He was also still the Celtics' starting center.

His first year running the team marked the end of the Celtics' glorious eight-year streak, but that could hardly be blamed on the coaching.

That year Wilt Chamberlain and a wondrous 76er team rose up and set a then-record 68 victories against just 13 regular season losses, and rolled to the NBA title.

But the Celtics bounced back to the top the next two seasons (once from the fourth seed), thwarting the Lakers yet again and proving that Russell was a champion no matter what he did.

Auerbach concurred, telling the Celtic Nation website, "Russell and Michael Jordan were the two greatest players to ever play the game. Russell made everyone play better. When it comes to winning, no one comes close."

And nobody probably will, until there's a three-handed center.

RUSSELLMANIA From 1957–69, the Boston Celtics captured 11 NBA titles, and sublime center Bill Russell (pictured with coach Red Auerbach) was the only man to play on each team.

WHEN THIS BEAR ROARED, IT USUALLY ENDED WITH A MAJOR TRIUMPH.

Jack Nicklaus

He started big, finished big, and stayed big all the way in between.

That's the way Jack Nicklaus played golf. The 1962 U.S. Open was the site for his first tour victory when, as a 22-year-old, he bested the great Arnold Palmer in a playoff to become that event's youngest-ever champion. More than two decades later, his final tour win offered even more drama, when a sizzling fourth round at the Masters earned him a sixth green jacket and made him the oldest player to capture a major.

Those triumphs bookended 16 other major crowns, and as the 2007 season dawned, Nicklaus remained the only golfer in history to win each of the majors—the PGA Championship and British Open being the others—at least three times.

His victory over Palmer, on Arnie's home course at Oakmont (Pennsylvania) no less, showed the nerves of graphite Nicklaus possessed. Afterward Palmer warned, "Now that the big guy's out of the cage, everybody better run for cover."

With his masterful power fade, Nicklaus became the longest hitter of his generation, but he also had amazing control and one of the tour's most dependable putting strokes, particularly when a match was on the line. He became the first player in history to capture back-to-back Masters, following up his runaway 9-stroke win in 1965 with a playoff victory over Gay Brewer and Tommy Jacobs.

By 1971 Nicklaus had won each of golf's Grand Slam events twice, and at the 1975 PGA Championship—played at Firestone Country Club in his native Ohio—he surpassed Bobby Jones's mark by capturing his 14th major. He then added the 1978 British Open title and in 1980 scored two more majors—the U.S. Open and a fifth PGA Championship—to bring his record-breaking total to 17.

He then went off course with a spell that saw him win just twice over the next five seasons, with no majors. And 1986 began no better— Nicklaus missed the cut in three of his first seven tour events and withdrew from another. Golf's next generation had seemingly pushed him into the shadows.

And although Nicklaus managed to reach the weekend at Augusta by shooting rounds of 74 and 71, no one had a sense he'd be a factor come Sunday afternoon. He began his final round 2 under par for the tournament and sat in eighth place, behind the formidable likes of Seve Ballesteros, Bernhard Langer, Nick Price, Tom Kite, Tom Watson, and third-round leader Greg Norman.

Even after a birdie on the 9th hole, Nicklaus lagged four shots behind the leaders. But in a flashback to his glory days, the Golden Bear roared again. He birdied the 10th and 11th holes by dropping putts of more than 20 feet; after bogeying number 12, he countered with a birdie on 13. On the par-5 15th, he slammed a 4-iron nearly 230 yards to set up an eagle. At the 175-yard 16th, he knocked a 5-iron within two feet of the cup.

When his caddie (his son Jackie) encouraged the shot with a "Be right" yell, Nicklaus confidently answered, "It is."

"It was one of those times where I hit the shot and as soon as it left the club, I knew exactly where it was," he said in a 2006 interview. "It was just sort of a cocky remark that I made. I don't normally make that. But I had so much confidence in what was going on, that's what I did."

By the time Nicklaus rolled in an 18-foot birdie putt on 17, he had moved atop the leader board; he then closed out his round with a par to card a 30 on the back nine. On Sunday. At Augusta. At age 46.

Norman, playing in the final group, made a patented charge of his own, shooting four straight birdies to pull into a tie. But the aggressive Australian bogeyed the 18th, leaving the green jacket to be placed around Nicklaus's shoulders for a final time.

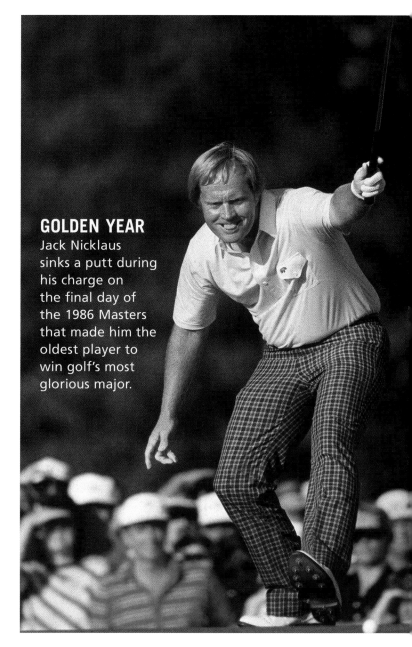

GOLDEN YEAR
Jack Nicklaus sinks a putt during his charge on the final day of the 1986 Masters that made him the oldest player to win golf's most glorious major.

**THOSE DAMN YANKEES
JUST KEEP ON WINNING.**

The New York Yankees

The New Yankees don't have droughts; the worst they ever have to suffer is a drizzle.

So goes the world when you reign as the quintessential sports dynasty. Entering the 2007 baseball season, the Yankees had won 26 World Series titles, which is not only more than twice as many as any other team, it's more than any other division. Even the number of Series they've lost (13) is staggering.

At first the Yanks needed to play a bit of catch-up in the trophy department; they didn't win their first championship until 1923, some 20 years after the introduction of the World Series. That happened to be the same year they moved across the Harlem River from the Polo Grounds into their own home—the stately 58,000-seat Yankee Stadium. They scored back-to-back Series wins in 1927-28, added another in 1932, and then captured four straight from 1936 to 1939. And that wasn't even their most impressive run: from 1949 to 1953 the Yankees won five consecutive World Series titles, all encased within an astonishing stretch where they were baseball's kingpins 10 times in 14 years. Even when they went through an elongated span without a title—from 1979 through 1995—they rushed back to the top with a flourish, capturing four crowns in five years, capped by a satisfying "subway series" triumph over the N.Y. Mets in October 2000.

On top of the championships is their sheer consistency: between 1926 and 1964, the Yanks strung together 39 consecutive winning seasons. They entered 2007 looking for a 10th straight American League East title. Never in history has the franchise suffered through more than four straight losing seasons.

There's little disagreement on the events that ignited this run to greatness. The timeline starts in 1915 when Colonel Jacob Ruppert and Captain Tillinghast L'Hommedieu Huston purchased the team, giving the Yankees an ownership that could compete financially with the rest of baseball. That was proven in 1920 when they obtained slugger Babe Ruth—who was just entering his prime—from the Boston Red Sox for $100,000 cash and a $300,000 loan.

PILING IT ON The 2000 Yankees celebrate their World Series triumph over the crosstown Mets, the 26th title in the history of the storied franchise.

With the Yankees suddenly outdrawing their Polo Grounds landlord and co-tenant New York Giants, and also reaching the World Series in 1921 and 1922, it came time for them to find their own home. Ruth fittingly hit the first home run in the new park, a three-run shot in a victory over the Red Sox, and would later rate that blast as his favorite of all. That's quite a distinction for a guy who had 713 others to choose from. The 1923 season ended with a six-game Series win over the rival Giants, with Ruth belting three round-trippers.

Ruppert became the team's sole owner that same year and continued to build the Yankees for long-term success. Ruth was joined by Lou Gehrig and fellow sluggers Bob Meusel and Tony Lazzeri to form the famed "Murderer's Row" lineup of 1927. Transitions were seamless with the likes of Joe DiMaggio, Bill Dickey, Lefty Gomez, and Red Ruffing working their way into the mix over the next 10 years. The next crop of superstars—which included Mickey Mantle, Yogi Berra, Johnny Mize, Phil Rizzuto, Roger Maris, Elston Howard, and Whitey Ford—carried the franchise into the mid-1960s. By the late 1970s, Reggie Jackson, Graig Nettles, Thurman Munson, Willie Randolph, Catfish Hunter, and Ron Guidry had taken center stage. The Yankees' recent run at the end of the 1990s was fueled by standouts Derek Jeter, Bernie Williams, Paul O'Neill, and Jorge Posada on offense and Roger Clemens, Andy Pettitte, and Mariano Rivera on the mound. Put this assemblage together and you have a Hall of Fame of Hall of Famers.

EVEL KNIEVEL **CRACKED** HIS OWN FORMULA FOR FAME.

Evel Knievel

NUMBELIEVABLE

For most sports stars, fame comes through broken records. For Robert Craig "Evel" Knievel, it was all about broken bones.

He had 35 of them...or maybe it was 40...or 53, depending on the story being spun. It doesn't matter except that with each failing jump, Knievel seemed to become more famous—an American icon who was equal parts P.T. Barnum and G.I. Joe.

Even if he never jumped, his life story could make an interesting TV miniseries—he owned the plane that billionaire Howard Hughes died in, spent two years as a roommate of actor Telly Savalas, and was in the same jail as Charles Manson.

Yet it was on a motorcycle—or being thrown from one—where most of the world learned of Knievel. His love of bikes and stunts came as a child from seeing Joey Chitwood's Auto Daredevil Show whenever it visited his hometown of Butte, Montana. At age 15 he received his first motorcycle, a BSA-125 Bantam, from his father.

Knievel, though, wasn't simply a biker. Physically talented and mentally tough, he developed into an exceptional athlete who won ski-jump competitions, ran track, and even played minor-league hockey for the Charlotte Clippers of the Eastern Hockey League. He was only 21 years old when he launched his own hockey team, the Butte Bombers. Artfully playing the role of showman and promoter, Knievel even convinced the vaunted Czechoslovakian Olympic team to come to Butte for a tune-up game before the 1960 Squaw Valley Games.

Following a mix of successful jumps and disastrous crashes, Knievel leaped into the headlines on New Year's Eve 1967 when he attempted to jump 151 feet across the famous fountains of Caesar's Palace in Las Vegas. What happened that day was spectacular on all fronts—the venue, the crash, and especially the fame.

With thousands looking on and the stunt being filmed for ABC's *Wide World of Sports,*

Knievel's cycle suddenly lost speed as it approached the ramp. He still cleared the fountains but landed awkwardly at the other end, causing him to fly over the bike, crash onto the pavement, and roll like a tumbleweed for several yards. Knievel broke his back and crushed his pelvis, and additionally fractured his hip, wrist, and both ankles.

"I got hurt real bad at Caesar's Palace," he told Don Gilbert in an article for *POPsmear* magazine. "Landed on my head. That was the most serious of all. I remember the whole thing, every tiny bit of it. There was a little six-foot safety ramp, and I landed right on top of it."

The accident left him in a coma and unconscious for nearly a month, but when he woke up, Knievel must have felt like he was living a dream. Overnight, he had become internationally famous.

His celebrity continued to grow, leading to a 1974 pay-per-view event in which he sought to jump Idaho's Snake River Canyon. But following hype usually reserved for a championship boxing match or a Super Bowl, the stunt was a dud. The parachute on his Skycycle X-2 deployed before he left the launch pad, causing Knievel to glide across the canyon, eventually bumping into the far cliff. Although he wasn't seriously hurt, he knew not much separated him from death that day.

Still, his fame continued to soar. In May 1975 at Wembley Stadium, in front of a crowd estimated at 100,000, Knievel attempted to jump 13 double-tiered city buses. He cleared 12—and shattered his pelvis. Before an ambulance could cart him off to the hospital, he grabbed a microphone and told the audience he was going to retire. But later that year he came back to perform a stunt that attracted the largest audience in the history of *Wide World of Sports*, sailing over 14 Greyhound buses at Kings Island amusement park in Ohio.

He then had his "jump the shark" moment—literally—in 1976. Knievel had planned to jump a tank of great white sharks on live TV at the Chicago Amphitheatre, but the daredevil crashed violently during a practice run and was forced to cancel the show.

After that, he made only occasional jumps, mostly with his son, Robbie, before retiring for good in 1981.

One of Knievel's favorite quotes during the height of his racing fame was, "A man can fall many times, but he is never a failure until he fails to get up." To prove the point, no matter how many times he fell, Evel Knievel always got up.

49-0

WHEN HE **ENTERED** THE RING, HE ALWAYS **LEFT** A WINNER

Rocky Marciano

So, 49 may not be the ideal, round number athletes would like to see in their career victory totals, but then again the round number that follows is completely perfect. Zero losses.

Rocco Francis Marchegiano, better known as Rocky Marciano, the Brockton Blockbuster, was the only world heavyweight boxing champion to walk away from the ring undefeated.

At 5'11" and 185 pounds, Marciano was by no means a giant, but he had a strong chin, a huge heart, and a powerful right hand. Forty-three of his 49 victories were by knockout, despite having the shortest reach—68 inches—of any heavyweight champion. He was the inspiration for Sylvester Stallone's enduring *Rocky* movies.

At 25, the Brockton, Massachusetts, native gave up his job as a digger for the gas company and became a full-time pro fighter after some AAU success. His early fights were mostly in clubs in Providence, Rhode Island, for purses around $40. But a thrilling two-round knockout victory over Pat Richards in his first fight in Madison Square Garden in late 1949 catapulted him onto the radar screen, and when he appeared on national TV for the first time in the summer of 1951, he knocked out Top-10 contender Rex Layne in six rounds. That led to a bout with childhood idol Joe Louis, who was well past his prime but came back to the ring to pay off back taxes to the IRS. The Brockton Blockbuster knocked out the Brown Bomber in the 8th.

"When Louis went down," said the Rock, "I was glad that he wasn't getting up. But then I remembered what a wonderful career he had, and I felt terribly sad instead of elated."

In 1952, more than five years after he started fighting professionally, Marciano was given a title shot, against 38-year-old heavyweight champion Jersey Joe Walcott in front of 40,379 fans at Philadelphia's Municipal Stadium. In the very first round, the wily Walcott knocked Marciano to the canvas. The pugnacious challenger sprang up to his feet as the referee counted four, ignoring trainer Charlie Goldman's advice to stay down till 8.

"Holy smokes, but I was surprised when he knocked me down," Rocky exclaimed after the fight. "I'd never been knocked down before, amateur or pro, and I'd often wondered what it would be like. I found out. It was sure nice to discover that I could get up with vision clear... Gee, but he's a tough old guy."

Finally, in the 13th round, the polite and persistent Marciano, trailing on the scorecards to the man 10 years his senior, was able to cleanly unload with a short right. Walcott went sprawling into the ropes and was counted out on a punch so hard that *Ring* magazine ranked it in the top three knockouts of all time.

ROCKABYE BABY The swan song of heavyweight champion Rocky Marciano's career, against the wily Archie Moore (left), had the same result as his 48 previous pro fights—with Marciano the winner.

After winning the title Marciano made six defenses over the next three and a half years, in a division mostly full of mediocrity and boxers past their prime. Still, Marciano took on all legitimate comers. The first was a rematch with Walcott. KO in the first.

Next up was Roland LaStarza, who had lost a controversial split decision to Marciano at the Garden in 1950. LaStarza was ahead on points for a while, but Marciano wore him down and sent him through the ropes in 11.

Then came Ezzard Charles, the former champion who had been relieved of his title by Walcott a few years before. The gutsy Charles went the distance with Marciano and lost in a decision, but was knocked out in their rematch three months later. Marciano knocked out British and European champion Don Cockell in nine rounds and concluded his career with a slugfest against Archie Moore.

"Actually, I had more than 49 fights," Marciano contended. "I was proud of being champion and I was determined never to get out of condition. So I boxed [sparred] 250 rounds before the Ezzard Charles fight, 250 before each of the Walcott fights, and 200 for the Don Cockell fight. And every round, even in training, was a real battle."

208

FAIRLY COMMON MEASURABLES
YET A VERY UNCOMMON CAREER

Jerry Rice

Common knowledge says that if you want to score touchdowns in the NFL, you should be a running back, a "red zone" rambler who slashes and surges behind a mountainous offensive line, occasionally picking up some one-yard cheapies—not a wide receiver. And even for a pass-catcher, Jerry Rice had common speed (4.5 seconds in the 40-yard dash) and common size (6'2", 200 pounds).

But once the whistle blew, as numerous burned, beaten, and befuddled defenders can attest, everything about the man was uncommon.

Over a 20-year career, with 13 Pro Bowl nods, the extraordinary Rice became the NFL's all-time leader in career touchdowns, with an unearthly 208 to his credit.

Not bad for someone who didn't play Division I football. Rice played his college ball in Itta Bena, Mississippi, at tiny Mississippi Valley State University, where he was a Division I-AA All-American, teamed up with quarterback Willie Totten. When draft day came in 1985, 15 teams passed on this small-school phenomenon, but the San Francisco 49ers made him a first-round pick.

Bill Walsh, the mastermind coach of the 49ers, explained to the *Los Angeles Times* his team's reasoning. "Jerry's movements were spectacular for a pass receiver, no matter the level," the coach said. "Even a casual fan looking at him on that [Mississippi] team would have asked, 'Who is that?'"

Joe Montana found out quickly, hooking up with the supernova Rice for 55 scores in a little under five seasons together. As a rookie, the bricklayer's son made a big splash, averaging 18.9 yards a catch. However, he only caught 3 touchdowns. The following year, he shredded defenses with league-leading totals of 1,570 receiving yards and 15 touchdowns.

But that was just an appetizer for the strike-shortened 1987 season, where Rice set up a home away from home—a nice little getaway called the "end zone." Twelve games played, 22

FLASH 80 Jerry Rice's relentless quest for the end zone made it seem as though he had super powers.

touchdown receptions, and one rushing touchdown. He led the league with 23 TDs and 138 points, and as far as touchdown catches went, the receiver in second place, Mike Quick of Philadelphia, had 11, marking the only time in NFL history that a category leader has *doubled* the total of his nearest competitor.

Rice was also ridiculously prolific in the playoffs, too. He helped cement the Niner Dynasty as the MVP in Super Bowl XXIII, with 215 receiving yards and a touchdown in the 20-16 squeaker over Cincinnati, and he followed that up by hauling in a record three scoring passes in the XXIV laugher over Denver.

When Rice began his career, the record for most career touchdowns in the NFL was 126,

held by Jim Brown. The most career touchdowns by a receiver was an even 100, by Seattle great Steve Largent. With the help of legendary quarterbacks Montana and Steve Young, Rice flat out destroyed both marks, catching 197 touchdown passes, en route to his 208. The other 11 came on running plays and one fumble recovery. He also surpassed the great Walter Payton's records for yards from scrimmage and all-purpose with 23,540 and 23,546, and he caught at least one pass in an astounding 274 consecutive games.

For Jerry Rice, the numbers don't lie, but they probably wouldn't mind lying down from sheer exhaustion.

408

Eddie Robinson

There was no winning at all costs, just a lot of winning.

That defined Eddie Robinson's 57-year tenure at Grambling State, where he became one of the most admired figures in sports. By the time he retired at the end of the 1997 season, he had 408 victories—more than anyone in the history of college football—and his name had become inseparable from the school.

"When you say Coach Robinson, you say it all as far as Grambling is concerned," said Robert Piper, who played for Robinson and later became the school's Director of Athletics.

For his part, Robinson lived life without regret. "If I had to do all over again, I would do the same thing," he said in 2001. "I would come to Grambling, stay in Grambling, coach in Grambling."

The son of a sharecropper, Robinson was raised in Baton Rouge and graduated from Leland College in 1941. Shortly thereafter he took the only job he was to hold, immediately embracing the ideals of a school formed for African American youths in northern Louisiana. Back then it was still known as the Louisiana Negro Normal and Industrial Institute, and for a salary of $63.75 per month, Robinson coached football, basketball, and baseball; cut and lined the football field; and directed the girls' drill team at halftime. Following road games, he wrote stories for the local paper. Yeah, you know the line about doing everything but making the popcorn.

In 1942 his team went 9-0 and did not surrender a point, and in time he raised Grambling football to the "Notre Dame of Black Colleges," until all-white schools finally opened their doors to African American student athletes. Robinson's teams captured 17 SWAC titles and nine national championships, and he suffered through just five losing seasons. More than 200 of his players went on to the NFL, including Hall of Famers Willie Brown, Willie Davis, Charlie Joiner, and Buck Buchanan. He also coached Doug Williams, the Super Bowl XXII MVP, who took over the program upon Robinson's retirement.

Milestone wins included the 1976 Pioneer Bowl, when his Tigers beat Morgan State in the first game in Japan between American colleges. In 1984 Robinson registered his 315th collegiate win—passing Amos Alonzo Stagg—and a year later he recorded victory number 324 to eclipse Bear Bryant for the all-time collegiate mark. His 400th triumph, over Mississippi Valley State in 1995, was televised nationally.

Robinson was selected to the College Football Hall of Fame in 1997, the same year the Football Writers Association of America renamed its annual Coach of the Year award in his honor. Grambling's football stadium now bears his name as well. It's not a surprise that those who knew him want his name and legacy to remain in the public's consciousness.

"In athletics, we always say the way you play the game is the way you'll live your life," insisted Robinson. "Our motto was whatever you compete in or do, try to be the best."

Even at age 75, Robinson was working to make the young men in his program the best—and didn't want to stop. "I can't imagine myself settling down or just looking around. I'd have to do something," he told *The Boston Globe* in 1994. "I would probably still go around and encourage the kids. Let them know that they can be president of the United States. You have to believe that. This country is too big to dream small."

He finally did step down in 1997, though he kept his promise and traveled across the country as a goodwill ambassador for the school. Six years later, St. John's University (Minnesota) head coach John Gagliardi passed Robinson for the wins record.

"Eddie did things the right way," said Gagliardi, who entering the 2007 season had won 443 games en route to four Division III National Championships. "I look at it like I do a big game: sometimes you would like to see a way for both teams to win. He did so much for race relations and for black football."

And through football, Eddie Robinson did even more for America.

A GRAMBLING MAN For better than 50 years, Eddie Robinson coached the Grambling football team to national prominence.

511

CY YOUNG'S PITCHING PROWESS TOOK THE BASEBALL WORLD BY STORM.

Denton True Young

Yeah, but he lost 316 games, too.

That could be a cynic's only retort upon hearing of Cy Young's never-to-be-broken major league standard of 511 victories. That's 5-1-1. To understand how untouchable the mark is, a pitcher could win 30 games for 17 straight seasons and still come away a victory shy. Then remember that no pitcher has won 30 games since 1968.

Denton True Young was born on an Ohio farm in 1867 and knew he had a gifted arm from an early age. "All of us Youngs could throw," he said. "I used to kill squirrels with a stone when I was a kid, and my granddad once killed a turkey buzzard on the fly with a rock."

The PETA vote aside, Young would become one of baseball's most popular figures as the game pushed into its modern era. Known for a rubber arm even by that day's standards—when pitchers regularly made 40 or more starts per season—he earned his nickname while impressing scouts during a game with Canton of the Tri-State League.

"I thought I had to show all my stuff, and I almost tore the boards off the grandstand with my fastball," he said of the 1890 incident. "One of the fellows called me 'Cyclone,' but finally shortened it to 'Cy,' and it's been that ever since."

Later that year, in his major league debut for the Cleveland Spiders, he handcuffed the hard-hitting Chicago Colts on just three hits while taking an 8-1 decision. "Can Young pitch?" the *Cleveland Leader & Herald* rhetorically asked the next day. "Can a fifer fife?" was the reply.

He spent eight seasons with the Spiders, during which time the mound was reset from 50 feet to its current distance of 60 feet, six inches from home plate. The move was barely noticeable in Young's stat line; he won 36 games with a 1.93 ERA and 168 strikeouts in 1892 (before the switch) and won 34 with a 3.36 ERA and 102 strikeouts in 1893 (after the switch).

Young and the franchise relocated to St. Louis in 1899, but after two seasons there—unhappy with his contract and disliking the Midwestern city's hot summers—he opted for more money

($3,000 per year), a different city, and even a new league. He signed with what would become the Boston Red Sox of the American League, a move that only enhanced his fame.

Also part of the Young legacy is that he threw the first pitch in the first World Series, played in 1903 between Boston and National League champion Pittsburgh. Uncharacteristically, he was hit hard and touched for four runs on three hits in the opening frame of an eventual 7-3 loss. He regrouped to win his next two starts as Boston captured baseball's inaugural "fall classic." The highlight may have come in Game 5, an 11-2 Boston win, when he yielded two unearned runs and struck out four without a walk. At the plate, Young contributed a pair of hits and drove in three runs.

The following season he threw 24 consecutive hitless innings—still a major league record. Within that streak came the first perfect game of the 20th century and the first in the history of the American League. Longtime Philadelphia A's manager Connie Mack, whose team failed to hit Young's offerings that day, maintained it was the "greatest exhibition of pitching ever performed." That season also showed how refined a pitcher Young had become. In 1891, his first full year in the bigs, he produced 147 strikeouts, but also walked 140. In 1904 he sent down 200 batters, yet yielded a paltry 29 free passes.

On August 13, 1908, in recognition of his contributions to baseball, the pitcher was feted with a "Cy Young Day" at Boston's Huntington Avenue Grounds. All American League games were canceled and instead a league All-Star team came to town for an exhibition game that attracted a crowd of more than 20,000. Young, moved by the show of affection, was presented several gifts, among them a key to the city of Boston.

Yet as Reed Browning wrote in his book *Cy Young: A Baseball Life*, "The most extraordinary gesture of all was [Boston team owner] John Taylor's: he gave the entire gate of $7,500, a sum greater than Young's salary for the year, to his star hurler."

Historians have long theorized what made Young so dominant on the mound. One belief is that he took advantage of the soft baseballs that stayed in play for an extended period.

"Young rarely asked an umpire for a new ball, because he could make lopsided or scuffed balls dance like an ant on a hot stove," wrote Derek Gentile in his book *Baseball's Best 1,001*.

He also focused on conditioning, not pitching, before the regular season. "I had a good arm and legs," Young said. "When I would go to spring training, I would never touch a ball for three weeks. Just would do a lot of walking and running. I never did any unnecessary throwing. I figured the old arm had just so many throws in it, and there wasn't any use wasting them."

Young made one last throw to celebrate the 50th anniversary of the World Series. Before the start of Game 1 of the 1953 series between the Yankees and Brooklyn Dodgers, the 85-year-old Young tossed out the ceremonial first pitch to Yankees catcher Yogi Berra. It was a strike.

714/755

THE GREATEST HOME RUN HITTERS **OF ALL TIME** SHARE SOME SURPRISING SIMILARITIES

Babe Ruth/Hank Aaron

One was bombastic. The other was relentless. One was the home run. The other was a homebody.

One was the Pablo Picasso of his day, wildly talented and expressing himself in ways that nobody had conceived of before. The other was Norman Rockwell, a master craftsman who was taken for granted while churning out masterpiece after masterpiece.

One was a showman, the most famous person in the country, who cracked wise about the president's salary in comparison to his own. The other was a quiet gentleman who was overshadowed by flashier ballplayers in his day and had to face the specter of ignorant Jim Crow racism.

Babe Ruth and Hank Aaron were the two most prolific home run hitters of the 20th century and seemed to be polar opposites, in both style of play and personality. However, closer examination of their careers, in addition to these contrasts, reveals parallels that aren't immediately obvious:

All-Around Athletes

Of course, both Aaron and Ruth are synonymous with the home run, but they were extremely versatile and gifted all-around players. Each man wound up as an outfielder after displaying great talent at another position.

Ruth was an All-Star pitcher with the Boston Red Sox, who pitched 29⅔ consecutive scoreless World Series innings—a record that stood for 43 years. "Ruth made a grave mistake when he gave up pitching," fellow Hall of Fame outfielder Tris Speaker quipped. "Working once a week he might have lasted a long time and become a great star."

Aaron began his career in professional baseball, after not playing high school ball, as a gifted shortstop for the Negro League's Indianapolis Clowns. "He's a natural-born ballplayer. God done sent me something," said Clowns manager Buster Haywood.

Philosophy of Slugging

George Herman Ruth, born in Baltimore, Maryland, was listed at 6'2", 215 pounds, but anybody who's seen photos of the Bambino in his heyday, the late 1920s, knows that the scale groaned a little more than that. Henry Louis Aaron, born in Mobile, Alabama, was a lithe and compact 6', 180 pounds, with wrists of thunder.

Although the Babe was exponentially cockier than Aaron, each man knew he held a great advantage when in the batter's box.

> "How to hit home runs: I swing as hard as I can, and I try to swing right through the ball…The harder you grip the bat, the more you can swing it through the ball, and the farther the ball will go. I swing big, with everything I've got. I hit big or I miss big. I like to live as big as I can."
>
> —Babe Ruth

> "The pitcher has got only a ball. I've got a bat. So the percentage in weapons is in my favor, and I let the fellow with the ball do the fretting."
>
> —Hank Aaron

Ruth Ran Roughshod

In 1919, his last year with the Boston Red Sox, Babe Ruth led the American League in home runs with a brand-new single-season record of 29. After Boston owner Harry Frazee foolishly sold Ruth, the Bambino explosion began in earnest. In 1920, Ruth smashed his year-old record by walloping 54 home runs, surpassing every other team in major league baseball except the Philadelphia Phillies.

Over the course of his career, he led the league in home runs 12 different times and established the single-season mark on four occasions. He rang up his career total of 714 home runs (708 in the American League) in only 8,399 official at-bats, which means that he hit home runs 8.5 percent of the time, still the best career pace by far.

Such was the magnitude of his prowess that his foes were awestruck and appreciative just to witness it. "I hope he lives to hit 100 homers in a season," said Frank "Home Run" Baker. "I wish him all the luck in the world. He has everybody else, including myself, hopelessly outclassed."

Aaron's Marathon of Mauling

If Babe Ruth was a time bomb at the plate for opposing pitchers, Hank Aaron was water torture. Although he led the NL in homers four times (1957, 1963, 1966–67), Hammerin' Hank never reached the 50 home run plateau in a single season, considered the benchmark for sluggers. His career high was 47.

But in a storied 23-year career, the relentless Aaron had double-digit home run totals in every season and became an even more proficient long-ball threat as he got older. The only two times he led the league in home run percentage were when he was 37 and 38 years old. His homers generally weren't gargantuan blasts of the Ruthian variety, but the respect for what he could do at the dish was universal.

The story goes that teammate Rico Carty had been mercilessly struck out three times in a game by the great Sandy Koufax, and he confronted the Hall of Fame lefty afterward to ask if he was angry at him for some reason. "Young man, I don't even know you, but as long as you're hitting in front of Henry Aaron, you're going to have a tough time with me," Koufax said.

Strange Coincidences

They each scored exactly 2,174 runs, tied at the time for second place behind Ty Cobb. Rickey Henderson has since moved into first place on the list. Absurdly, Ruth and Aaron each won their league's MVP award just once apiece—Babe in 1923 and Aaron in 1957.

The Chase

Babe Ruth chased nobody. Massive 19th-century star slugger Roger Connor of the New York Giants and St. Louis Cardinals held the previous career high water mark with a piddling 138 home runs, which Ruth blew by in his third full season as a starting outfielder, to very little fanfare. If you want to get technical about it, that meant that Ruth wound up setting a new all-time home run record on each of his final 576 home runs.

Four decades later, as Aaron steadily moved up the home run list, entering the 1973 season with 673 round-trippers, the specter of Ruth's giant shadow dimmed what should have been a celebratory period. Sadly, just as it had been for Roger Maris in the nerve-wracking 1961 season,

Aaron had to deal with much more than athletic pressure. Then, it had simply been negative feelings toward Maris because he was threatening an icon. However, in Aaron's case, the situation was much worse, as racism reared its ugly head. He received 930,000 pieces of mail in 1973, some of the letters encouraging and friendly, but a large percentage of them were hateful and sometimes contained death threats.

In a 1999 interview with *American History* magazine, Aaron said, "The only thing I can say is that I had a rough time with it. I don't talk about it much. It still hurts a little bit inside because I think it has chipped away at a part of my life that I will never have again. I didn't enjoy myself. It was hard for me to enjoy something that I think I worked very hard for. God had given me the ability to play baseball, and people in this country kind of chipped away at me. So, it was tough. And all of those things happened simply because I was a black person."

Amazingly, under such pressure, the 39-year-old Aaron had one of his finest seasons in 1973, blasting 40 home runs in just 392 at-bats, to draw within one of the Babe. And happily, he was able to witness another side of the human spirit at his home field after he'd popped out in his last at-bat. When he reported to left field for the ninth inning, a strange thing happened, as he wrote in his autobiography, *I Had a Hammer*:

There were about 40,000 people at the game—the biggest crowd of the season—and they stood and cheered me for a full five minutes. I couldn't believe that I was Hank Aaron and this was Atlanta, Georgia. And God Almighty, all I'd done was pop up to second base...and to tell you the truth, I didn't know how to feel. I don't think I'd ever felt so good in my life. But I wasn't ready for it."

The Babe's sense of ceremony, showmanship, and self-assurance comes through in *The New York Times'* account of his record-breaking 60th home run (passing none other than his own total of 59), off Washington's Tom Zachary:

"While the crowd cheered and the Yankees players roared their greeting, the Babe made his triumphant, almost regal tour of the paths. He jogged around slowly, touched each bag firmly and carefully...The Babe's stroll out to his position was the signal for a handkerchief salute in which all of the bleacherites, to the last man, participated. Jovial Babe entered into this carnival spirit and punctuated his kingly strides with a succession of snappy military salutes."

Conversely, it was a decidedly different tone the night of April 8, 1974, when Al Downing of the Dodgers tried to sneak a fastball by Hank Aaron. No. 44 slammed it into the bullpen, into the glove of teammate Tom House, and into the ages. In Aaron's own words:

"I was in my own little world at the time. It was like running in a bubble and I could see all these people jumping up and down and waving their arms in slow motion...I was told I had a big smile on my face as I came around third. I purposely never smiled as I ran the bases after a home run, but I suppose I couldn't help it that time."

No matter what future sluggers do to the record books, the numbers 714 and 755 will always have deep meaning to baseball fans. Although Ruth and Aaron were exceedingly different men, this anecdote from the voluble Babe's past covers their legacies pretty well:

A reporter was talking to Babe a few years down the road about the last game of the 1928 World Series, when he had slammed three home runs. "Gee," the reporter said, "A good day for you, eh?"

"Yeah," Babe replied. "I had a good day. But don't forget, the fans had a hell of a day, too."

5,714

Nolan Ryan

NOLAN RYAN EXPRESSED HIMSELF WITH STRIKEOUTS.

Was anyone really surprised to see Nolan Ryan turn up as a pitchman for Advil?

After all, for the better part of 27 major league seasons, the fireballing righty had thrown pills and caused headaches for sluggers ranging from Roger Maris to Mark McGwire. For his career—which began in 1966 with the Mets and included stops with the Angels, Astros, and Rangers—Ryan struck out a staggering 5,714 batters, far and away the most in baseball history.

How Ryan intimidated opposing batters is legendary. In high school, he is said to have fractured one batter's arm and cracked another's helmet on back-to-back pitches. He gave one major leaguer a concussion after hitting him with a change-up.

Detroit Tigers first baseman Norm Cash felt so overwhelmed that he once carried a wooden piano leg to the plate to face Ryan. Even Reggie Jackson—he of the October swagger and 563 career home runs—admitted being "scared" to bat against the "Express." Then there's Rickey Henderson, Ryan's 5,000th strikeout victim,

who once bragged, "If you haven't been struck out by Nolan Ryan, you're nobody." (Of course someone should have mentioned that to Fernando Valenzuela, the 1981 NL Rookie of the Year and himself an accomplished hurler, who never fanned in 11 career plate appearances against Ryan).

Born January 31, 1947, in Refugio, Texas, Lynn Nolan Ryan Jr. attended Alvin High School, where he was discovered by N.Y. Mets scout Red Murff. The team grabbed him in round 12 of the 1965 draft and Ryan soon after joined the minor league Marion Mets, where team president Robert Garnett recalls the pitcher's debut: "I'll never forget that first pitch. It knocked the catcher's glove off. He had the opposing team so scared, they were ducking coming out of the dugout."

Ryan began emerging from major league dugouts just one year later. And in 1968, his first full season in the bigs, he rang up 133 K's in 134 innings. He then helped the 1969 "Miracle Mets" to the World Series title, saving Game 4

EXPRESS DELIVERY In his 27-year major league career, fireballer Nolan Ryan struck out more batters than anyone in Major League history.

In 1980 Ryan made more history when he signed with the Astros and became baseball's first million-dollar player. While in Houston he broke Walter Johnson's major league strikeout mark and became the first pitcher to whiff 2,000 batters in each league. He then joined the Texas Rangers in 1989, where he immediately proceeded to strike out 301 batters, his sixth season with 300 or more K's.

Ryan fired his final pitch on September 22, 1993, at the age of 46. When he retired, he held or shared more than four dozen MLB/AL/NL records...not surprisingly, one of them was for wild pitches (277). Another, though, was for no-hitters (7), and he padded his resume with 12 one-hitters. He also won 324 games.

But when one thinks of Nolan Ryan, it will always be about strikeouts. And many of the 1,176 different major leaguers he fanned still get pains whenever they think of facing him. Advil anyone?

against the Orioles, but two years later was shipped to the California Angels in exchange for infielder Jim Fregosi. Listen closely and you'll still hear the shrieks of regret echoing throughout the Shea Stadium corridors.

His first season in California was beyond spectacular: Ryan became the first righty since Bob Feller to fan 300 batters, won 19 games, and backed it all up with a 2.28 ERA. And that was just the start. In 1973 he threw a pair of no-hitters and struck out a major league-record 383 hitters. He reached 300 strikeouts again in 1974, the same season he was clocked unleashing a 100.9 mph fastball against the Minnesota Twins.

Unequaled Pitchman

Nolan Ryan's 27-year career is a record for longevity among major league baseball players. In this category, he edges out catcher Deacon McGuire (1884-88, 1890-1908, 1910, 1912) and pitcher Tommy John (1963-74, 1976-89), who each played 26 seasons. The only athlete to last longer in a major team sport was Gordie Howe, who spent 32 years in pro hockey (1946-80) playing in the NHL and WHA. George Blanda owns pro football's record, with 26 years of service in the NFL and AFL.

18,355

Emmitt Smith

NUMBELIEVABLE

Emmitt Smith wouldn't have been nearly as good in *Flashdance*. It's not his style.

Smith—the NFL's all-time rushing leader and, more recently, champion of ABC's *Dancing with the Stars*—has always been more about substance.

"He's the best north-south runner I've ever seen," lauded Jimmy Johnson, the former Dallas Cowboys head coach who selected Smith with the 17th overall pick in the 1990 NFL draft.

While runners with more jukes and more speed grabbed more headlines, nobody grabbed more yards than Smith, who earned his reputation by becoming a workhorse you could look to on any down, in any situation, and anywhere on the field.

Somehow, 16 NFL teams did look right past the 5'9", 209-pound Smith. It was their loss, thought Hall of Fame receiver Michael Irvin, who knew the Cowboys had unearthed a gem the first time he met the University of Florida running back.

"The first thing he said to me—and we were not a good team at the time—was he wanted to win Super Bowls. And he did that," recalled Irvin after Smith supplanted Walter Payton as the league's career rushing leader. "He said he wanted to win rushing titles, and he did that. He said he wanted to win MVPs, and he did that. His last goal, which I thought was a fantasy, was to become the all-time leading rusher in the NFL. And today he did that."

Long before that day came, Smith rehabilitated a proud Dallas franchise that had fallen on hard times. The Cowboys, an anemic 1-15 the year before Smith arrived, improved to 7-9 with his addition to the backfield. By his second year they were 11-5 and heading toward three Super Bowl championships. Smith garnered MVP honors at Super Bowl XXVIII against the Bills after rushing for 132 yards and scoring two second-half touchdowns that keyed the 30-13 win.

Smith captured three straight NFL rushing titles between 1991 and 1993 and added a fourth in 1995, when he dashed for a career-high 1,773 yards. For 11 consecutive years, he topped the 1,000-yard mark, the first player in NFL history to do so. During the height of his football prowess, Smith also fulfilled a promise to his mother, completing his undergraduate studies and earning a degree in public relations.

On October 27, 2002, at age 33, Smith eclipsed Payton's mark of 16,726 yards in a game against the Seattle Seahawks.

He left Dallas after that season and signed with Arizona, but five games into his Cardinals career broke his shoulder blade. That in and of itself was news—in 13 years with Dallas, Smith missed a total of four games due to injury. Even more disheartening, the injury occurred back in Dallas against the Cowboys. Smith returned healthy in 2004 and piled up 937 rushing yards, pushing his career total to 18,355.

With that effort—and believing he had made the point that he could still play in the league when many questioned his ability—Smith decided it was time to retire. He signed a ceremonial one-day contract with the Cowboys in February 2005, leaving the game not only with the rushing mark, but also with 164 rushing touchdowns, highlighted by a 25-touchdown season in 1995.

"I'm going to be biased when you ask me, 'Who's the greatest running back of all time?'" acknowledged Moose Johnston, Smith's blocking back for many of those Dallas teams. "You can probably make a case for eight to 10 guys. But for me, it's always been Emmitt."

After wowing NFL audiences for all those years, Smith wowed the judges and viewers of

Dancing With The Stars in 2006, a reality-television talent competition that pairs a celebrity with a professional dancer. He teamed with Cheryl Burke to win the show's third-season crown. Incidentally, he "outperformed" another NFL legend, Jerry Rice, who had been a runner-up in the show's second season.

In the long-running rivalry between the Cowboys and 49ers, chalk this one up to the guy who wore a star on his helmet.

38,387

Kareem LOTS OF POINTS FROM POINT-BLANK RANGE

The skyhook sealed the deal. Makes sense.

If you're going to tear down one of the biggest records in NBA history, might as well use the heavy artillery for the job. That's precisely what Kareem Abdul-Jabbar did on April 5, 1984, when he lofted in his trademark shot, the skyhook, to eclipse the legendary Wilt Chamberlain as the player with the most points in league history. Chamberlain had racked up an amazing 31,419 points over his 14 years in the league.

But when the big, begoggled No. 33 flipped in a 12-footer over shot-blocking machine Mark Eaton, Wilt had to take an unaccustomed position—the back seat.

Kareem pushed the new standard to 31,421, and even though he was closing in on 37 years of age, there was still plenty more damage to be done to defenders around the league. The man whose Islamic name means "noble, powerful servant" played five more seasons after passing Wilt and put the record in the stratosphere, at 38,387 points.

His last coach, Pat Riley, famously raised a glass to someone he'd both won with, and lost to, during his playing days. "Why judge any more?" Riley asked. "When a man has broken records, won championships, endured tremendous criticism and responsibility, why judge? Let's toast him as the greatest player ever."

There are those who say that Michael Jordan was the greatest basketball player who ever came down the pike. The debate over the best center to play the game usually comes down to Wilt or Bill Russell. But Riley's case has merit—it truly would be hard to come up with much evidence to the contrary if you were to name the 7'2", 267-pound Kareem Abdul-Jabbar as The Man in either category. The three-time UCLA All-American took the pros by storm right from the start and ended his storied 20-year NBA career having scored more points than anyone else had, or probably ever will.

CAPTAIN HOOK On the way to six NBA titles and six MVP awards, Kareem Abdul-Jabbar also scored the most points in league history, with 38,387.

Sources

Chapter 1

-18

"I wasn't the pioneer..."
Bob Carter, "Tiger's decisive '97 Masters win was historic" (ESPN.com, June 23, 2006), http://espn.go.com/classic/s/add_woods_tiger.html

Author John Feinstein compared the unprecedented accomplishment to "a rookie in baseball hitting .600."
"Year of the Tiger" (The Online NewsHour, June 23, 2006), http://www.pbs.org/newshour/bb/sports/tiger_4-14.html

"I would compare this to Jackie [Robinson]. To me, a black winning a major golf championship is just as high as that."
Ron Green Jr., "Lee Elder Lives Dream through Tiger Woods' Win" (tigertales.com, April 3, 2007), http://www.texnews.com/tiger/green041497.html

20

With good reason, most of the city's sports....
"Seattle Mariners vs. Boston Red Sox" (Baseball Almanac, January 17, 2007), http://www.baseball-almanac.com/box-scores/boxscore.php?boxid=198604290BOS

"I watched perfect games by Catfish Hunter and Mike Witt, but this was the most awesome pitching performance I've ever seen."
"Roger Clemens" (BaseballLibrary.com, January 24, 2007), http://www.baseballlibrary.com/baseballlibrary/ballplayers/C/Clemens_Roger.stm

29' 2½"

"When I went to the top of the runway...."
"Approaching the Unreachable" (The New York Times, May 29, 1987), www.nytimes.com

59

"People ask me if I thought I was going to shoot a 59..."
"Not much happened right away [when I shot 59]...."
"Somebody could do it tomorrow. Half of me expects somebody to break the record any time and the other half..."
Gary D'Amato, "Geiberger's 59 Began As a Matter of Survival" (JS Online, January 24, 2007), http://www2.jsonline.com/golfplus/jun02/48626.asp

63

"Go kick it."
Chris Pike, "Where Are They Now? Tom Dempsey" (NewOrleansSaints.com, January 24, 2007), http://www.neworleanssaints.com/newsroomarticle.cfm?articleid=1099

"I knew I could kick it long enough..."
Chuck O'Donnell, "Tom Dempsey—The Game I'll Never Forget" (FindArticles.com, January 27, 2007), http://www.findarticles.com/p/articles/mi_m0FCL/is_10_32/ai_102656419

3:59.4

"It may seem incredible now that the world record at this classic distance could be set by an amateur athlete, in bad weather, on a university running track..."
"Reliving the Breaking of the Four-Minute Mile Barrier" (Univer-

sity of Oxford, April 6, 2007), http://www.admin.ox.ac.uk /po/news/2003-04/feb/06a.shtml

"My body had long since exhausted all its energy, but it went on running just the same..."
Roger Bannister, The Four-Minute Mile (Guilford, CT: The Lyons Press, 2004).

10.0
"Nadia Comaneci: Fearless and Tireless" (The New York Times, July 25, 1976), www.nytimes.com

Chapter 2

17-0
"Okay, old man. Get those cataracts in motion. Turn up that hearing aid and let's go."
Edwin Pope, "17-Oh" (Super Bowl XLI Game Program, February 4, 2007), p. 244.

"If we lose this game, I'll kill you."
Ray Didinger, "Sudden Impact" (Super Bowl XLI Game Program, February 4, 2007), p. 136.

"Perfection ends a lot of arguments."
"The 1972 Miami Dolphins" (Phins.com, January 25, 2007), http://www.phins.com/72phins

61*
"It would have been a helluva lot more fun if I had not hit those 61 home runs."
Tom Seaver with Marty Appel, Great Moments in Baseball (New York: Carol Publishing Group, 1992).

72-10
"It's hard to translate..."
Clifton Brown, "Greatness Can See Bulls in the Mirror" (The New York Times, January 21, 1996), www.nytimes.com

86-1
"Even though I'd never heard of her, and couldn't pronounce or spell her name, I could tell she'd be trouble."
John Feinstein, "Final Bow" (2006 US Open Magazine, August 28, 2006), p. 135-36.

"Do you know the difference between involvement and commitment?"
"Martina Navratilova Quotes" (Brainy Quote, April 6, 2007), http://www.brainyquote.com/quotes/authors/m/martina_navratilov a.html

130
"This Is Rickey Henderson: Speed That Terrorizes" (The New York Times, December 16, 1984), www.nytimes.com

.406
"When I came to bat for the first time that day, the Philadelphia catcher, Frankie Hayes, said..."
"Bill McGowan Obituary" (Baseball Almanac, January 30, 2007), http://www.baseball-almanac.com/deaths/bill_mcgowan_obitu-ary.shtml

2,003
Before the season, the back had announced...
Joe Garner, And The Fans Roared (Naperville, IL: Sourcebooks, Inc., 2000).

Chapter 3

33
"33! A streak to remember" (SI.com).

47
"Men, the only people who never lose are the ones who never play the game."
Jim Dent, "Sooner Duster 47 Straight Opponents" (ESPN.com, January 30, 2007), http://espn.go.com/classic/s/2001/0823/ 1243043.html

56
"I never really felt any pressure. I was just a kid. I didn't know what pressure was, and I was having too much fun."
"DiMaggio's 61-Game Hitting Streak, Pacific Coast League" (The American Experience, February 1, 2007), http://pbs.org/wgbh/ amex/dimaggio/peopleevents/pande07.html

"That's when I became conscious of the streak. But [even] at that stage, I didn't think too much of it."
Harvey Frommer, "Joe DiMaggio's 56-Game Hitting Streak Began May 15, 1941" (Harvey Frommer on Sports, February 1, 2007), http://www.travel-watch.com/jd56game.htm

88
After Notre Dame's John Shumate hit a shot over Walton and then got a lay-up off a steal, it...
"100 Years Remembered in 100 Days" (University of Notre Dame Official Athletic Site, January 30, 2007), http://und.cstv.com/ sports/m-baskbl/spec-rel/011705aab.html

"What bothered me about the loss...was how we lost and the fact we went dead in the final three minutes."
Ray Marquette, "88 Consecutive Wins" (The Sporting News,

January 30, 2007), http://www.sportingnews.com/archives/sports-2000/numbers/139123.html

107

Larry Schwartz, "Moses Made Winning Look Easy," (ESPN.com), http://espn.go.com/sportscentury/features/00016350.html

2,130/2,632

"Only Lou's willingness and lack of conceit..."
William C. Kashatus, Lou Gehrig—A Biography (Westport, CT: Greenwood Press, 1959).

"Tonight, I stand here overwhelmed as my name is likened with the great and courageous Lou Gehrig. I'm truly humbled to have our names spoken in the same breath."
"Baseball's 25 Greatest Moments" (The Sporting News, February 12, 2007), www.sportingnews.com

"Breaking Lou Gehrig's record had nothing to do with extraordinary talent, which I don't have...."
Cal Ripken Jr. and Mike Bryan, The Only Way I Know (New York: Penguin Books, 1997).

Chapter 4

3

"He was Elvis and John Wayne and Steve McQueen and Christa McAuliffe all melded into one bad SOB."
Marty Smith, "Dale Footage Is Unbelievable, Unbelievably Moving" (ESPN.com, February 5, 2007), http://sports.espn.go.com/rpm/columns/story?seriesId=2&columnist=smith_marty&id=2740035

"We took that penny and glued it on the dashboard."
Leigh Montville, At the Alter of Speed (New York: Doubleday, 2001).

"Yes! Yes! Yes!" he exclaimed to an adoring crowd. "Twenty years! Can you believe it?"
Steve Waid, "At Last Earnhardt Wins Dayton 500" (The Earnhardt Connection, February 7, 2007), www.daleearnhardt.net/history/98daytona/index.htm

42

"If they expected any miracles out of [me], they were sadly disappointed...."
"Then I thought of Mr. Rickey—how his family and friends had begged him not to fight for me and my people..."
Jackie Robinson As Told to Alfred Duckett, I Never Had It Made (New York: Putnam, 1972), p. 46, p. 70, p. 72.

Chapter 5

1/8

"Man, I felt like Babe Root [Ruth]."
Darren Rovell, "Short on Size, Long on History" (ESPN.com, February 5, 2007), http://espn.go.com/mlb/s/2001/0816/1240553.html

Three-peat

"It's sort of been an interesting phenomenon..."
"What the Trojans Won't Do: Three-Pete" (ESPN.com, December 23, 2005).

4-4-4

"Moses Helps Dr. J, Sixers Reach Promised Land" (NBA.com), http://www.nba.com/history/finals/19821983.html

Fab 5

"From what the media has told me..."
"Michigan's Fab Five: Ready, Steady, Go" (The New York Times, April 6, 1992) www.nytimes.com

6'4³⁄4"

"When I got drafted, I knew I had a God-given ability..."
Larry Platt, "Charles Barkley" (Salon.com), http://archive.salon.com/people/bc/2000/05/30/barkley/print.html

"He gets rebounds that no one has ever gotten..."
"Charles Barkley's Outrageous Career" (Sports Illustrated, May 3, 1993), http://sportsillustrated.cnn.com/si_online/flashbacks/barkley/barkley_flashback/

#17 at TPC Sawgrass

"I'm going to be honest...there's not much about that day I remember. I kept hitting shots and they kept going into the water. It's a good hole. I just had a very bad day."
Garry Smits, "Treasure Island: Sawgrass' No. 17 Like No Other Hole on Tour" (golf.com, February 5, 2007), http://golfguide.cnnsi.com/gdc/news/article.asp?id=21650

"I once stood on the 17th tee with a six-shot lead and was still worried about getting it across..."
Ron Whitten, "Acquired Tastes" (Golf World, February 5, 2007), www.golfdigest.com/newsandtour/index.ssf?/newsandtour/gw200050318tpc.html

"We needed good, quality sand for developing the fairways. As the holes started developing..."
Mark Cubbedge, "Sawgrass' 17th: How a Legend Was Built" (TPC Sawgrass Club News, February 5, 2007), http://tpc.com/daily/sawgrass/news/how_a_legend_was_built.html